For Phoebe Jane

Library of Congress Cataloging-in-Publication Data

Richards, Roy.
    101 science tricks : fun experiments with everyday materials / Roy
Richards : illustrated by Alex Pang.
        p.   cm.
    Originally published: London : Simon & Schuster, c1930.
    Includes index.
    Summary: Presents 101 experiments and activities involving such
scientific principles as aerodynamics, light and color perception,
and optical illusion.
    ISBN 0–8069–8388–4
    1: Science—Experiments—Juvenile literature.   2. Scientific
recreations—Juvenile literature.   [1. Science—Experiments.
2. Experiments.   3. Scientific recreations.]   I. Pang, Alex, ill.
II. Title.   III. Title: One hundred one science tricks.   IV. Title:
One hundred and one science tricks.
Q164.R53 1991
507.8—dc20

               91–13263
                   CIP
                   AC

10 9 8 7 6 5 4 3 2 1

Published in North America in 1991 by
Sterling Publishing Company, Inc.
387 Park Avenue South, New York, N.Y. 10016
Originally published in Great Britain by
Simon & Schuster Ltd. Text © 1990 by Roy Richards
Illustrations © 1990 by Simon & Schuster
Distributed in Canada by Sterling Publishing
c/o Canadian Manda Group, P.O. Box 920, Station U
Toronto, Ontario, Canada M8Z 5P9
Printed in Hong Kong by
Wing King Tong Co Ltd.
All rights reserved

Sterling ISBN 0–8069–8388–4

101 SCIENCE TRICKS

FUN EXPERIMENTS WITH EVERYDAY MATERIALS

ROY RICHARDS

Illustrated by Alex Pang

Sterling Publishing Co., Inc.   New York

CONTENTS

1
on Looking

INTRODUCTION

People say that seeing is believing, but have you ever really thought about the way you see things?

Sometimes things aren't what they seem!

In **On looking** you'll find lots of fun experiments to do with mirrors and with the way you see things.

Did you know that you can use mirrors to make a periscope to peek over walls and around corners to find out what is happening? That's just what a submarine does. It raises a special tube called a periscope up out of the water to find out what is happening without being seen.

How about surprising your friends with some optical illusions? There are lots of things that you can do to make pictures move. You can get a dancer waltzing, a frog leaping or a dolphin jumping. Moving pictures like these were the beginning of films. And there are many other ways of creating illusions to surprise your friends.

It is easy to see from the illustrations and the instructions what you need to make the things, but look also at the special instructions on page 101 for handling knives and other tools safely. You may want to get a parent or teacher to help you with some projects.

MIRROR PLAY

Use a mirror.

1 Look at the sky. Be careful. Do not look at the sun.

2 Look around corners with your mirror.

3 Look behind you. What can you see?

4 Use your mirror to look over walls.

5 Write your name on a large piece of paper. Look at it in a mirror.

JUST ONE MIRROR

Take a small mirror, the kind you find in a woman's handbag.

Put it along each dotted line in turn, shiny side facing each picture, as shown in the picture on the left. What happens?

Make some designs of your own.

Put your mirror here

- - - - - - - - - - - - - - -

DICK

MARY

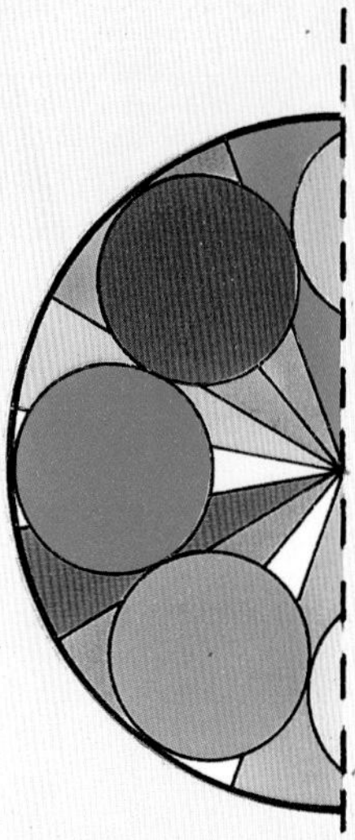

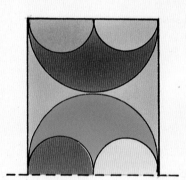

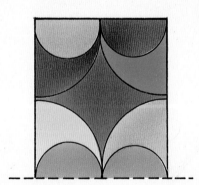

1 Symmetry is sameness on both sides of a center line. Our faces, for example, are pretty much the same on both sides of our noses. They have vertical symmetry. Try your mirror on one.

2 Examine the letters of the alphabet below. Which have vertical symmetry? Which have horizontal symmetry? Which have both? Which have none?

Put your mirror vertically down the center of the letter A.

The letter A has vertical symmetry.

Try it on the letter B.

It does not work for the letter B.

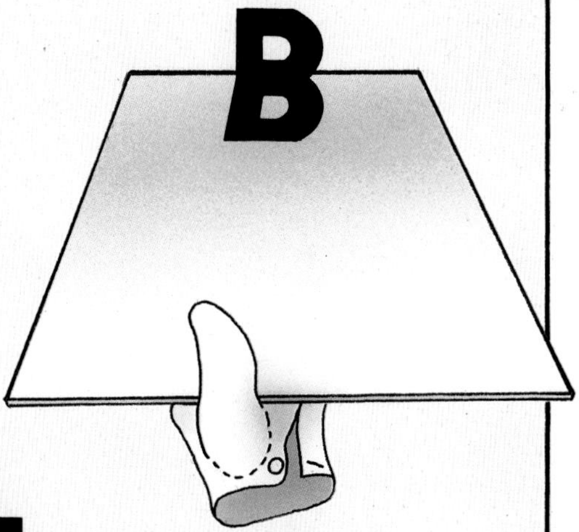

Try the mirror horizontally across the letter B.

Now it works! The letter B has horizontal symmetry.

ABCDE
FGHIJK
LMNOP
QRSTU
VWXYZ

HAT

MUM

symmetrical words

CHOICE

TRY TWO MIRRORS

1 Join two mirrors with cellophane tape as below.

2 Stand them up with the mirror fronts facing you.

3 Try your mirrors on each tortoise in turn. Place the mirrors on the dotted lines as shown, shiny sides facing on the tortoise. What happens?

4 Now try these patterns.

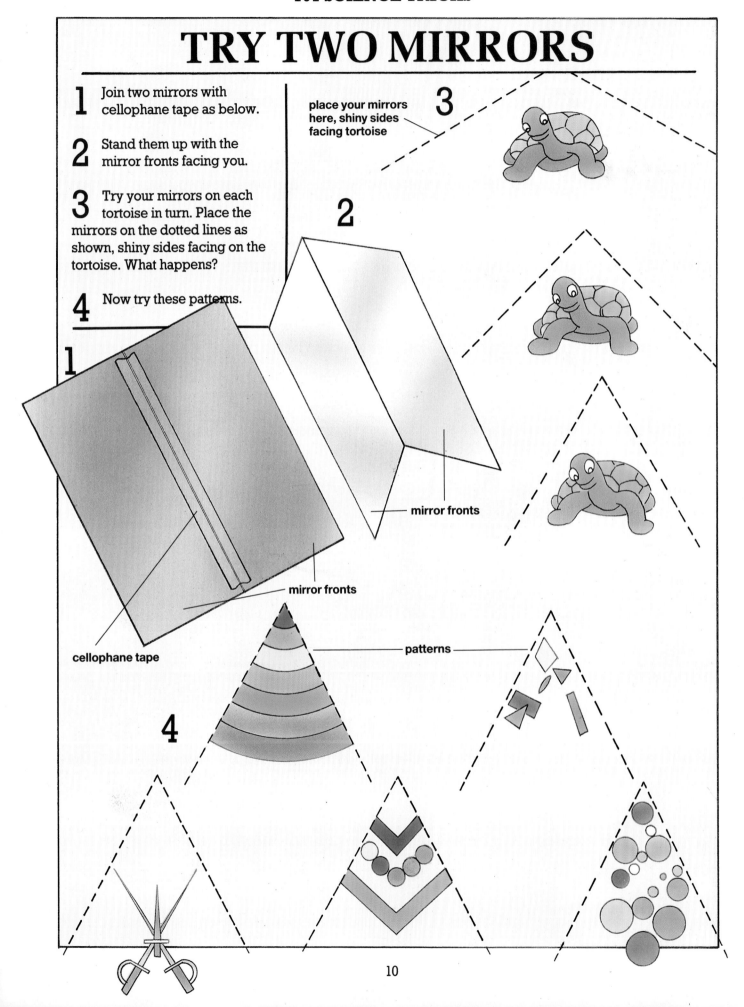

place your mirrors here, shiny sides facing tortoise

mirror fronts

mirror fronts

cellophane tape

patterns

KALEIDOSCOPE

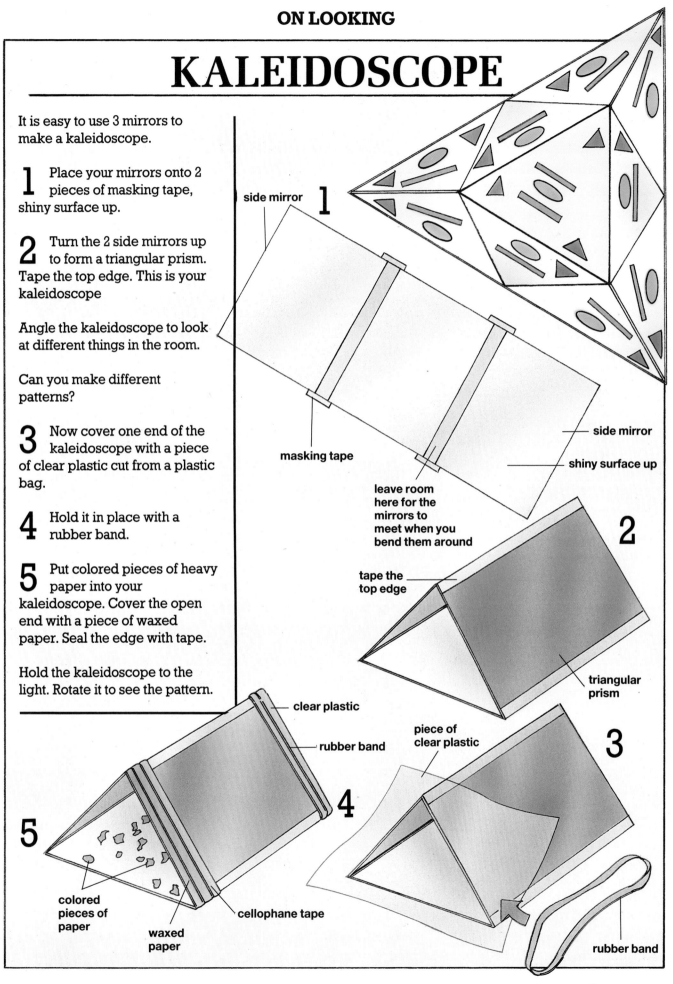

It is easy to use 3 mirrors to make a kaleidoscope.

1 Place your mirrors onto 2 pieces of masking tape, shiny surface up.

2 Turn the 2 side mirrors up to form a triangular prism. Tape the top edge. This is your kaleidoscope

Angle the kaleidoscope to look at different things in the room.

Can you make different patterns?

3 Now cover one end of the kaleidoscope with a piece of clear plastic cut from a plastic bag.

4 Hold it in place with a rubber band.

5 Put colored pieces of heavy paper into your kaleidoscope. Cover the open end with a piece of waxed paper. Seal the edge with tape.

Hold the kaleidoscope to the light. Rotate it to see the pattern.

side mirror

1

masking tape

side mirror

shiny surface up

leave room here for the mirrors to meet when you bend them around

2

tape the top edge

triangular prism

clear plastic

rubber band

piece of clear plastic

3

4

5

colored pieces of paper

waxed paper

cellophane tape

rubber band

11

PERISCOPES

Periscopes can be used to peek over walls or around corners. They can also be used to watch parades.

You will need two handbag mirrors to make a periscope and some long pieces of cardboard.

1 Cut a long piece of cardboard about 2½ times as long as the mirror but just as wide. Tape one of your mirrors to the middle of the cardboard, with the shiny surface facing up, and score the cardboard along the sides of the mirror.

2 Fold the cardboard into a triangular prism. Make sure you have a 90 degree angle where the ends meet. You may have to trim a tiny bit off each end. Keep the 2 b sides equal.

3 Do the same thing with your other mirror.

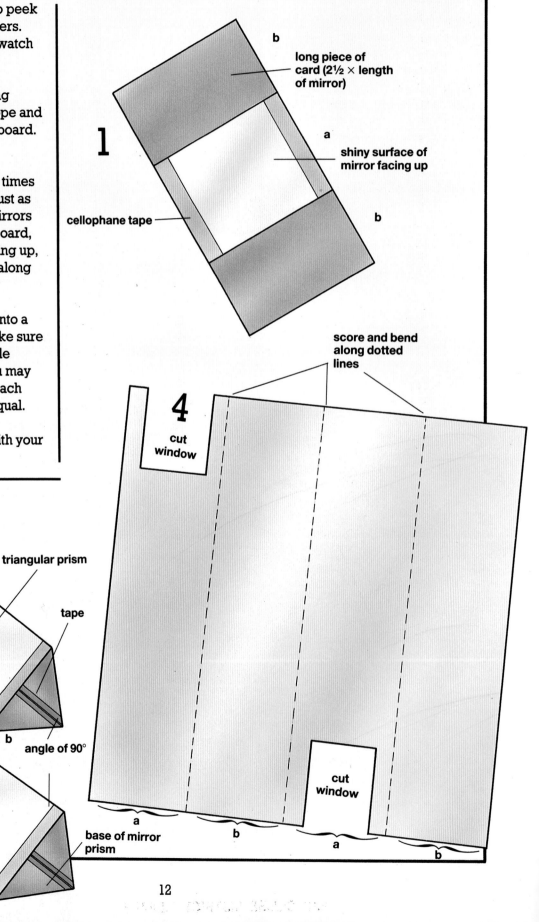

1

b

long piece of card (2½ × length of mirror)

a

shiny surface of mirror facing up

b

cellophane tape

b

score and bend along dotted lines

4

cut window

2

triangular prism

tape

a

shiny surfaces of mirrors

b

angle of 90°

3

base of mirror prism

cut window

a

b

a

b

4 Cut another long piece of cardboard as shown in the picture on the bottom right of page 12. Score your cardboard and bend it. Cut two windows. You are going to fold this to make the long tube shown in the two pictures below.

5 Make the long tube shown on the right. Its width and depth (a & b) must be the same as those of the base of your mirror prism. Join the edges with tape.

6 Put each triangular prism into the card tube so that the shiny surface of the mirror faces the window. Tape it in place.

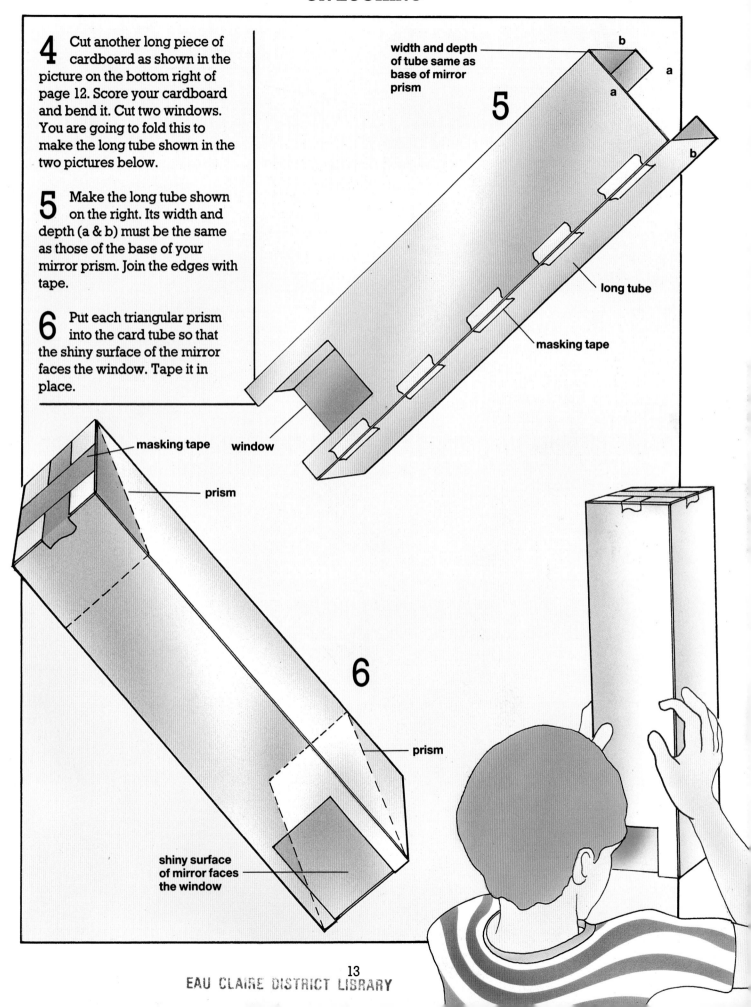

width and depth of tube same as base of mirror prism

b
a
a
b

5

long tube

masking tape

masking tape window

masking tape

prism

6

prism

shiny surface of mirror faces the window

SEEING IS BELIEVING

1 Cut out a piece of heavy paper the same size as the one immediately below or use a business card.

2 Place your card vertically along the dotted line between each of the pictures below. Put your nose on the top edge of the card as shown in the picture on the right. What happens?

Each eye receives a separate image. The brain merges these two images to make one picture. So the rabbit pops into its hutch or the spider into its web.

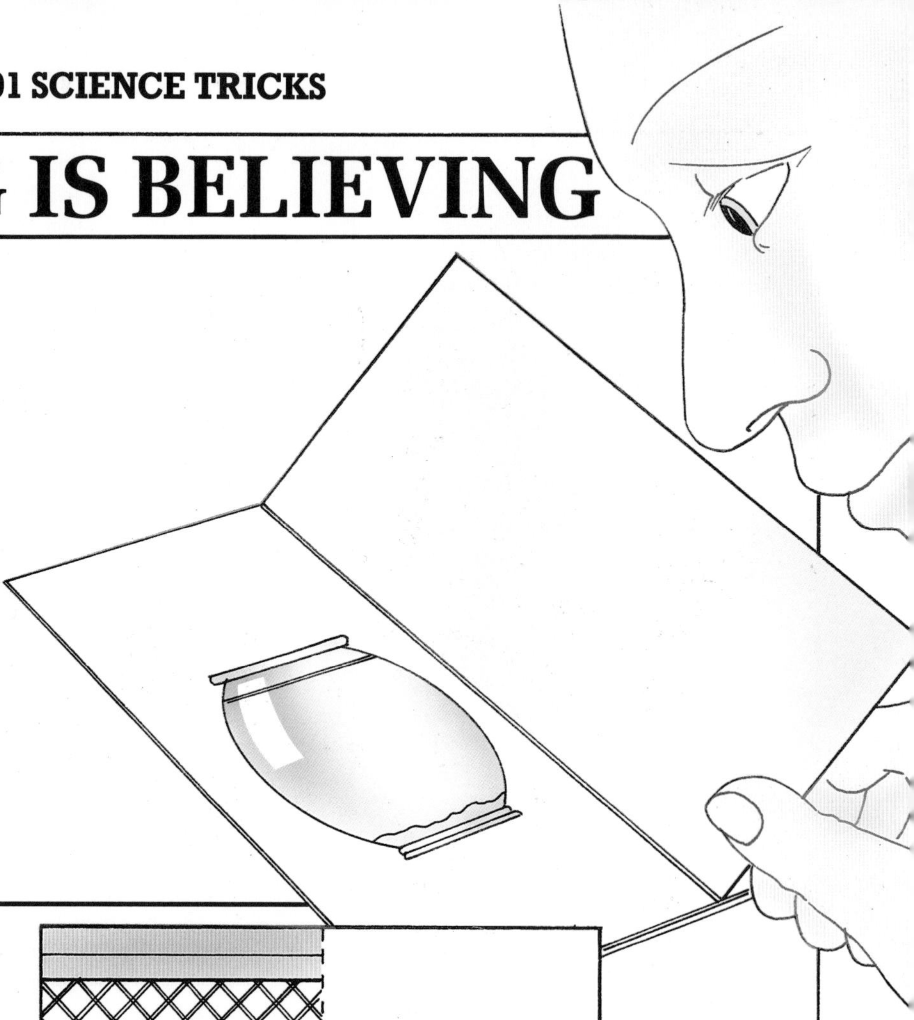

2³/₄"

1³/₄"

place your card vertically along the dotted line

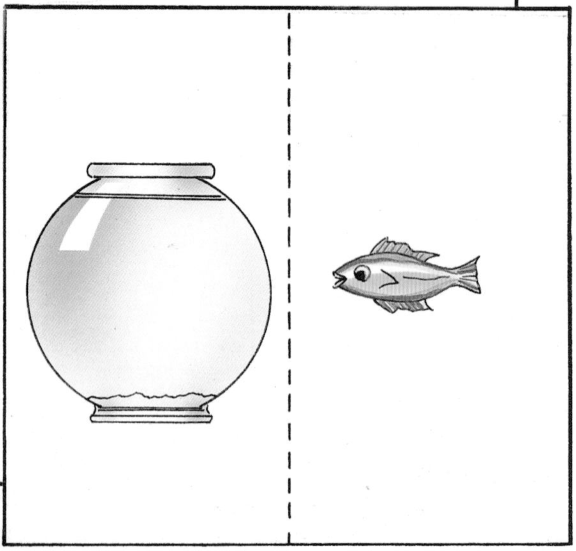

ON LOOKING

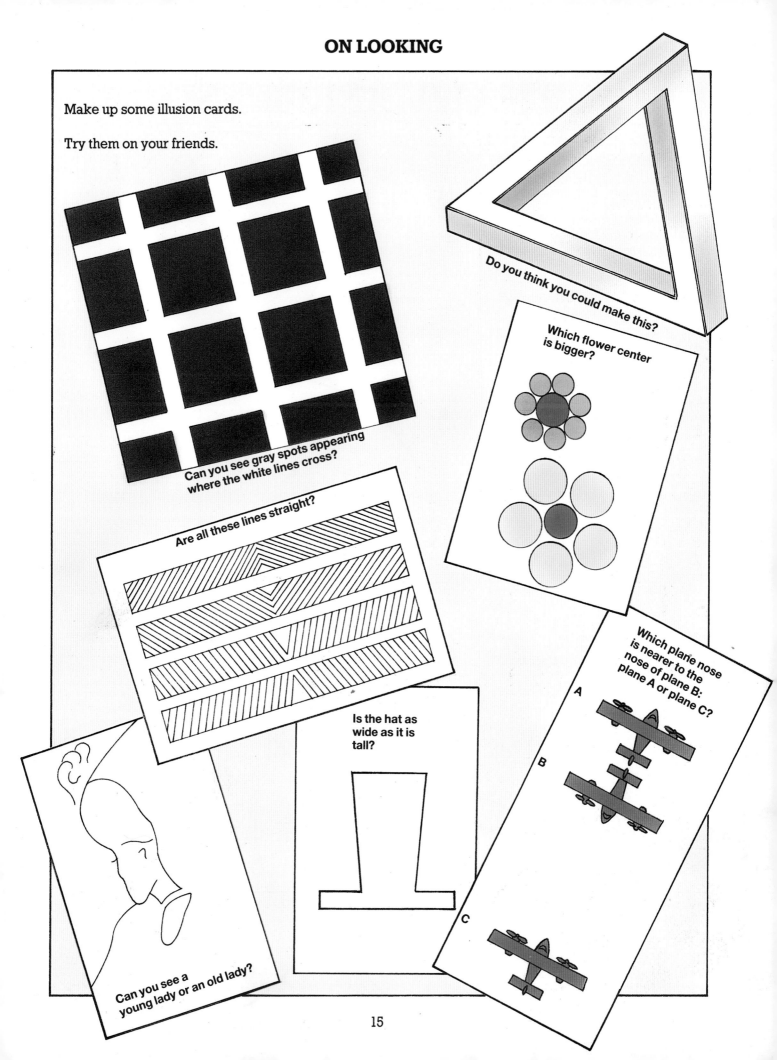

Make up some illusion cards.

Try them on your friends.

Can you see gray spots appearing where the white lines cross?

Do you think you could make this?

Which flower center is bigger?

Are all these lines straight?

Which plane nose is nearer to the nose of plane B: plane A or plane C?

A

B

C

Is the hat as wide as it is tall?

Can you see a young lady or an old lady?

THAUMATROPES

The thaumatrope was invented in 1826 and is one of the earliest optical toys. It is a spinning disc with a picture either side.

1 Cut a disc 3½ inches in diameter from cardboard like that on the back of a pad of paper.

2 Punch holes near the edge of the cardboard.

3 Thread string through the holes in the cardboard.

4 Draw pictures on each side of the cardboard circle. Remember to have the back picture upside down as is shown in the examples below.

5 Twirl the strings. The 2 pictures will merge as you spin the disc.

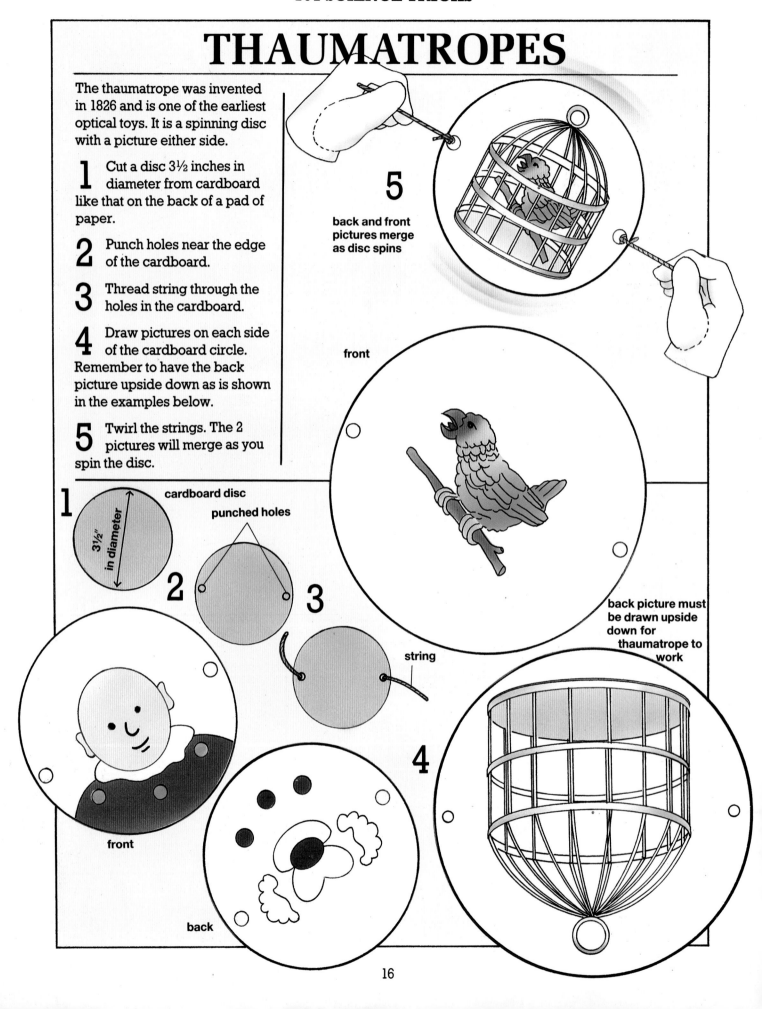

5 back and front pictures merge as disc spins

front

1 cardboard disc   3½" in diameter

2 punched holes

3 string

4 front   back

back picture must be drawn upside down for thaumatrope to work

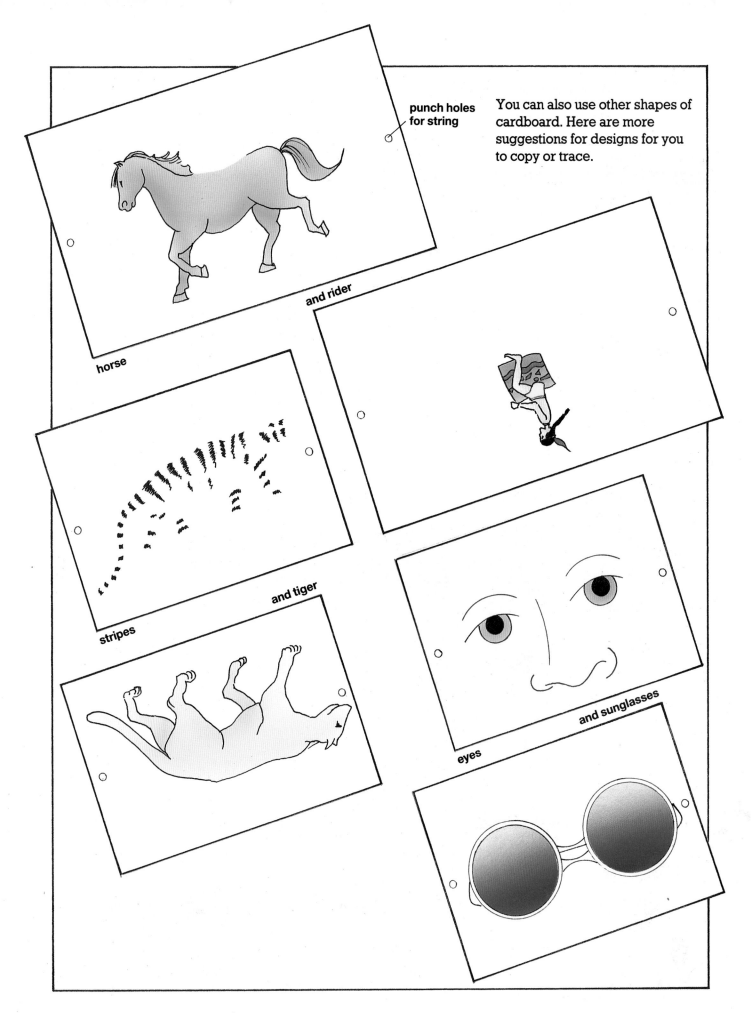

punch holes for string

You can also use other shapes of cardboard. Here are more suggestions for designs for you to copy or trace.

horse

and rider

stripes

and tiger

eyes

and sunglasses

PHENAKISTOSCOPES

Joseph Antoine Plateau, from Belgium, produced moving pictures by viewing a sequence of drawings through slits. The device he invented was called a phenakistoscope or stroboscope. It works because the brain has the ability to retain pictures for a short while. Each successive picture of the frog stays in your mind until the next replaces it.

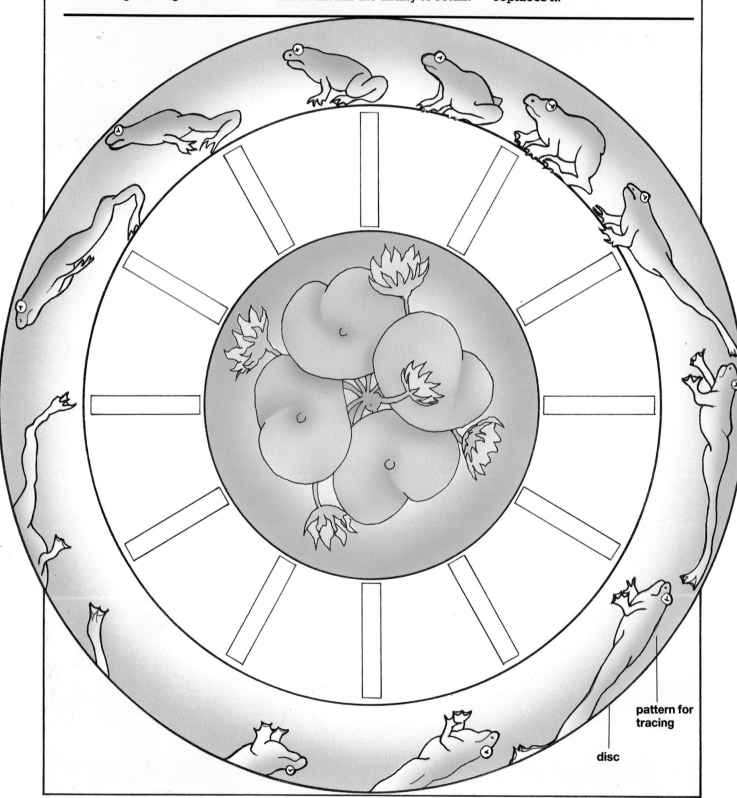

pattern for tracing

disc

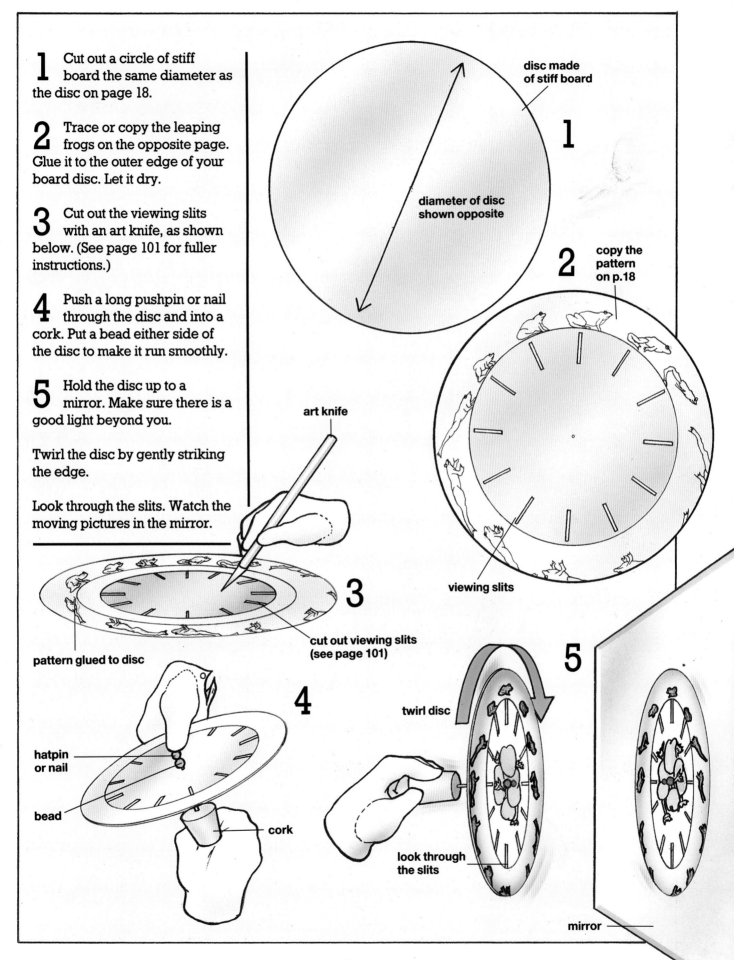

1 Cut out a circle of stiff board the same diameter as the disc on page 18.

2 Trace or copy the leaping frogs on the opposite page. Glue it to the outer edge of your board disc. Let it dry.

3 Cut out the viewing slits with an art knife, as shown below. (See page 101 for fuller instructions.)

4 Push a long pushpin or nail through the disc and into a cork. Put a bead either side of the disc to make it run smoothly.

5 Hold the disc up to a mirror. Make sure there is a good light beyond you.

Twirl the disc by gently striking the edge.

Look through the slits. Watch the moving pictures in the mirror.

disc made of stiff board

diameter of disc shown opposite

1

2 copy the pattern on p.18

viewing slits

art knife

3

pattern glued to disc

cut out viewing slits (see page 101)

4

hatpin or nail

bead

cork

5

twirl disc

look through the slits

mirror

19

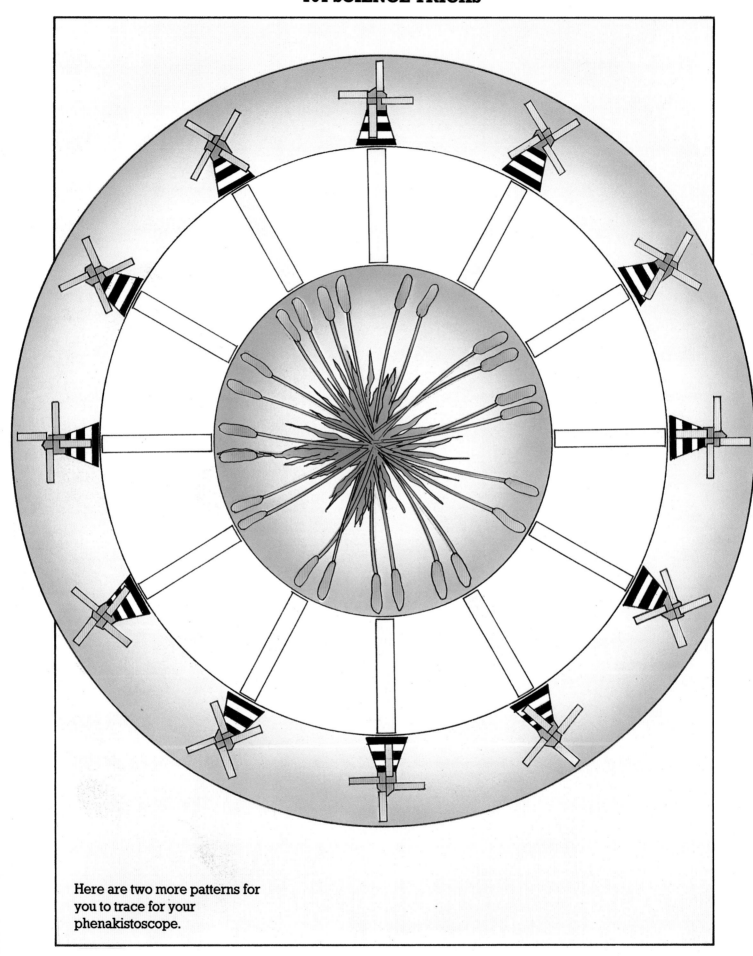

Here are two more patterns for
you to trace for your
phenakistoscope.

ON LOOKING

Look through the slits while spinning the disc slowly.

Now look while you spin the disc quickly.

What happens?

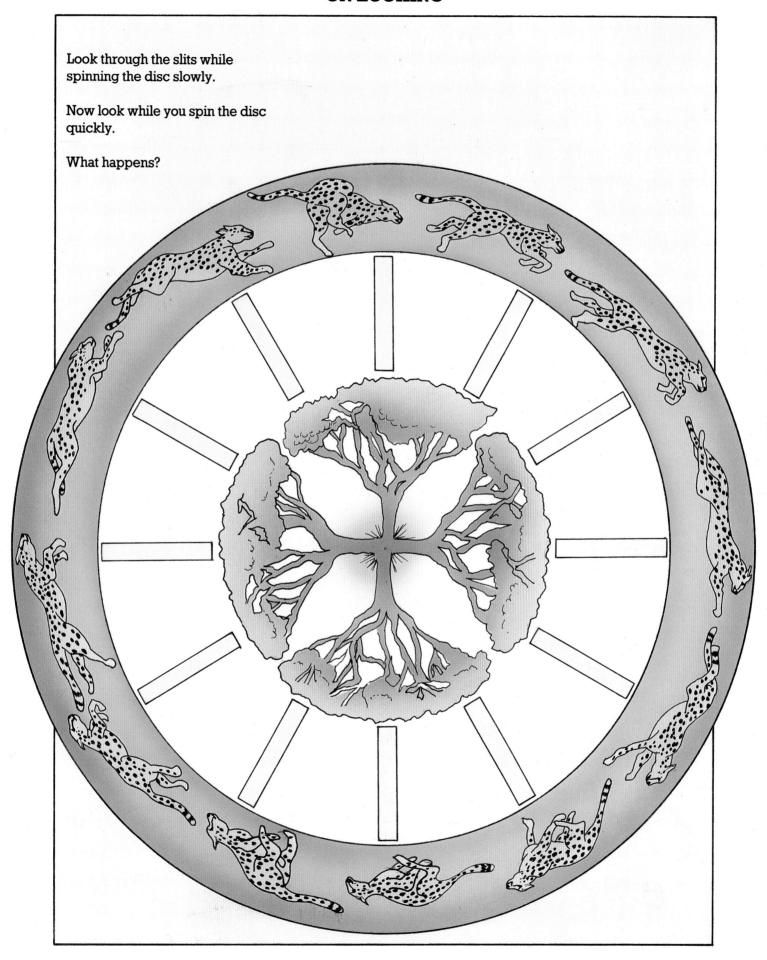

FLICK BOOKS

It is easy to make an action picture book. You need a story line like the one shown on the opposite page. It has 32 pictures. Copy the series of pictures shown on the opposite page onto heavy paper like a blank index card.

1 Cut out each picture. Punch two holes at the side.

2 Put them in number order, starting from the bottom. Put picture number 1 on the bottom and picture number 32 on top. Tie them with thin string. Bind with tape.

3 Hold the book by the bound end and flick the pages from back to front with your other hand. You will see the pictures move. Make up some more books. There are some suggestions below for story lines. You make up the "in between" pictures. Keep the pictures to the right.

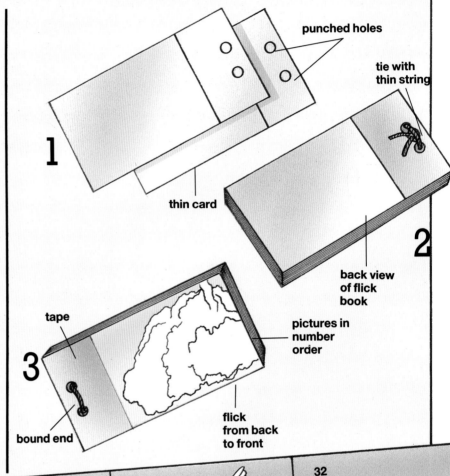

punched holes

tie with thin string

thin card

back view of flick book

1

2

tape

pictures in number order

3

bound end

flick from back to front

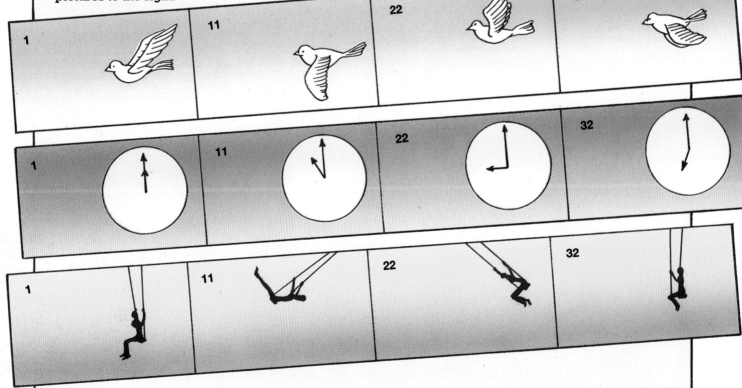

ZOETROPES

In 1834 William George Horner, an English mathematician, invented a device that became a popular toy. It enabled people to see moving pictures. You can make a zoetrope.

1 Draw a circle with a 3½″ radius on stiff, heavy paper. Cut out the disc.

2 Cut a thin strip of stiff, black paper 6¼″ × 22″. Use the template on the opposite page to give you the spacing for the slits and tabs. The slits must be cut out with an art knife (see page 101). You can cut the tabs with scissors.

3 Score along line AB and bend the tabs inward.

4 Glue the tabs to the disc. Join the overlap with cellophane tape.

5 Fix a pin through the center of the zoetrope (with a bead on either side so that it runs smoothly) into a cork. Stand the cork in a weighted bottle full of sand or soil.

You will need a strip of figures to stick inside your zoetrope. There are strips of figures for you to trace on page 25.

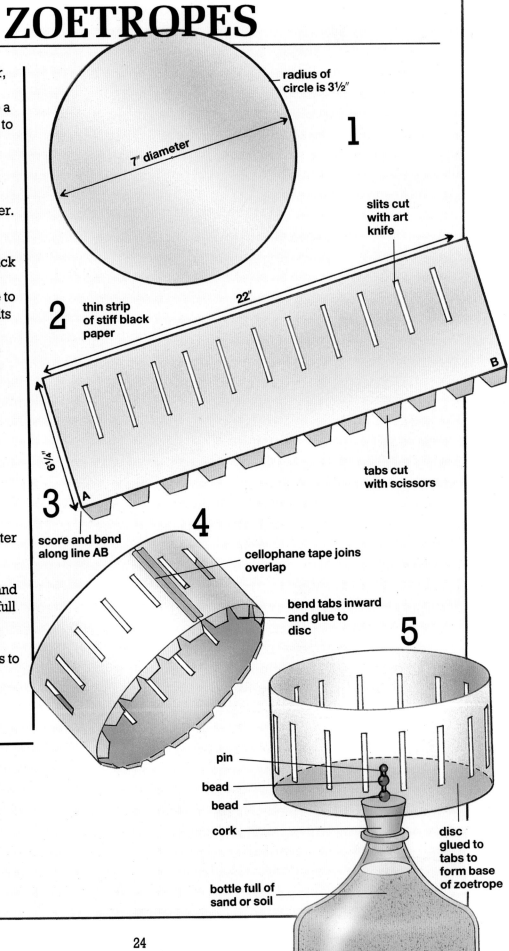

1 radius of circle is 3½″
7″ diameter

2 thin strip of stiff black paper
22″
6¼″
slits cut with art knife
tabs cut with scissors
A B

3 score and bend along line AB

4 cellophane tape joins overlap
bend tabs inward and glue to disc

5 pin
bead
bead
cork
disc glued to tabs to form base of zoetrope
bottle full of sand or soil

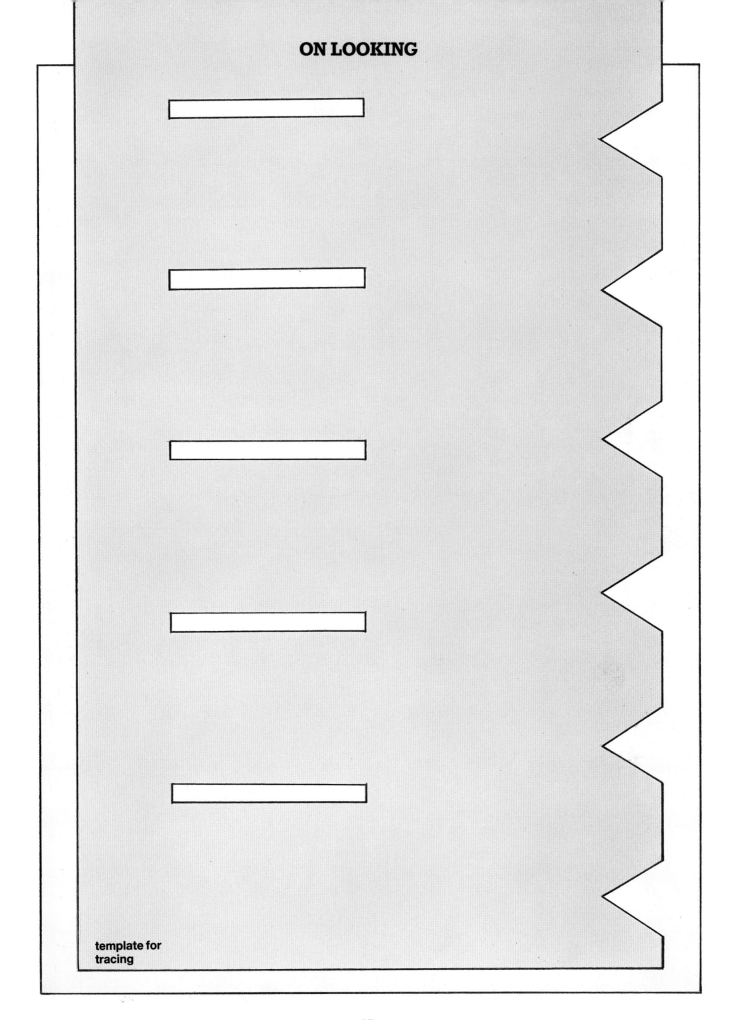

template for
tracing

101 SCIENCE TRICKS

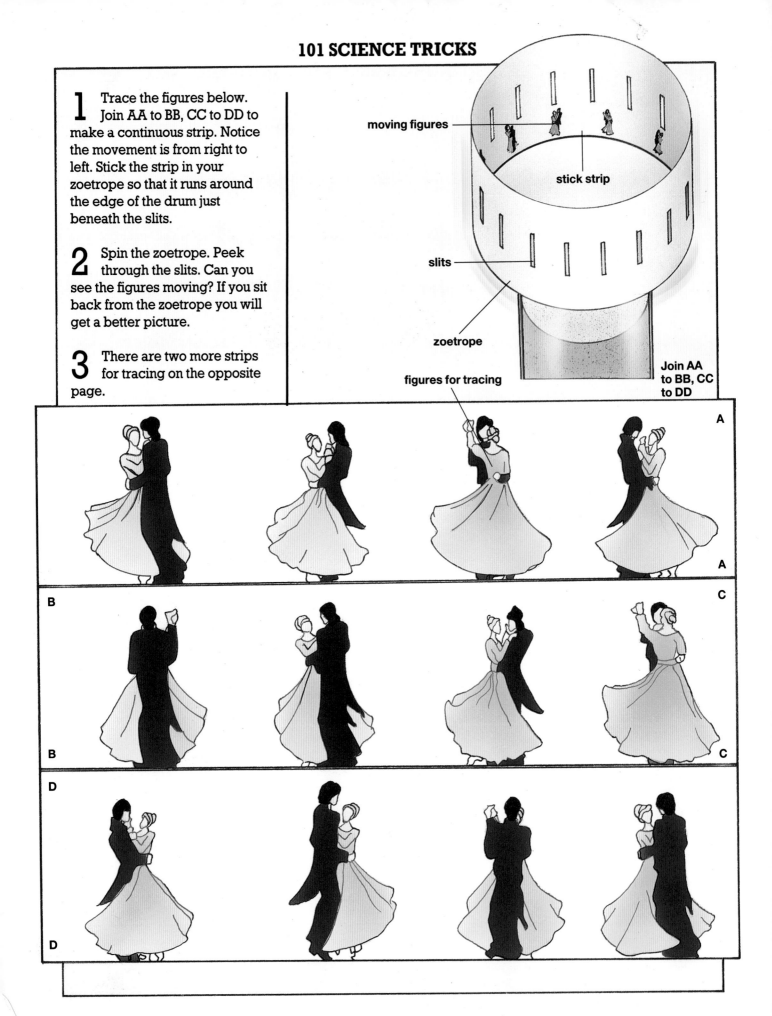

1 Trace the figures below. Join AA to BB, CC to DD to make a continuous strip. Notice the movement is from right to left. Stick the strip in your zoetrope so that it runs around the edge of the drum just beneath the slits.

2 Spin the zoetrope. Peek through the slits. Can you see the figures moving? If you sit back from the zoetrope you will get a better picture.

3 There are two more strips for tracing on the opposite page.

moving figures

stick strip

slits

zoetrope

figures for tracing

Join AA to BB, CC to DD

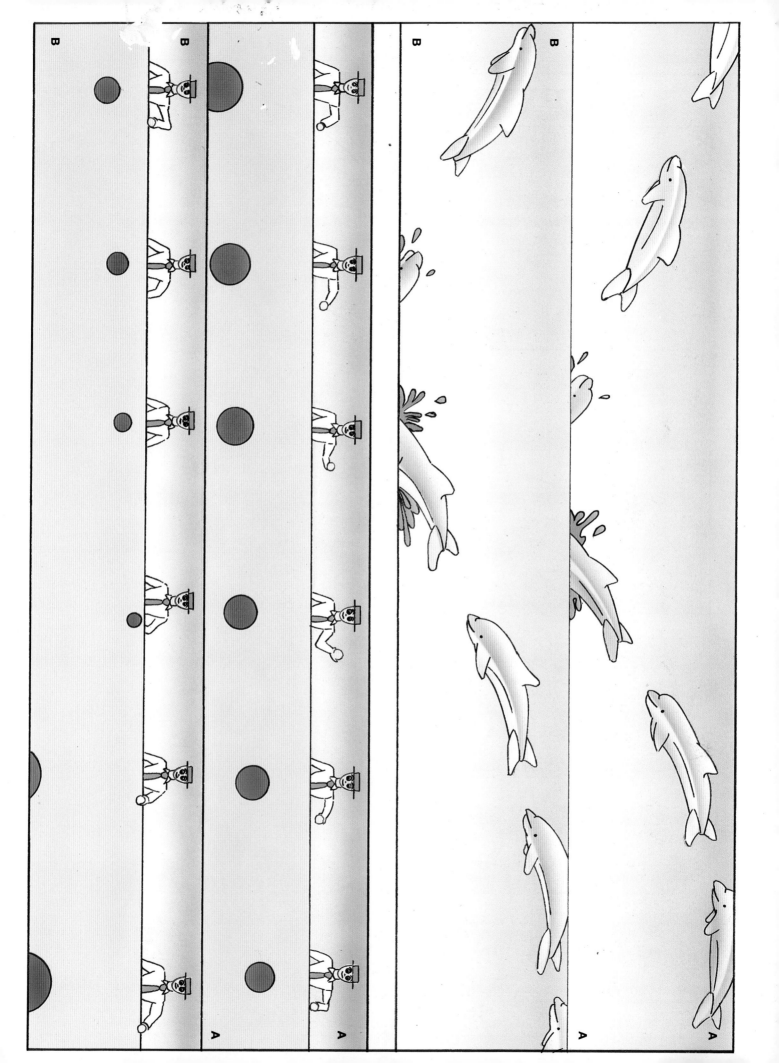

CURVES FROM CIRCLES

1 Take a compass and mark two points A and B, 4 inches apart.

2 Draw circles from each point. Increase the radius of each circle by ¼″ at a time.

3 Draw in ellipses as shown. Can you construct more?

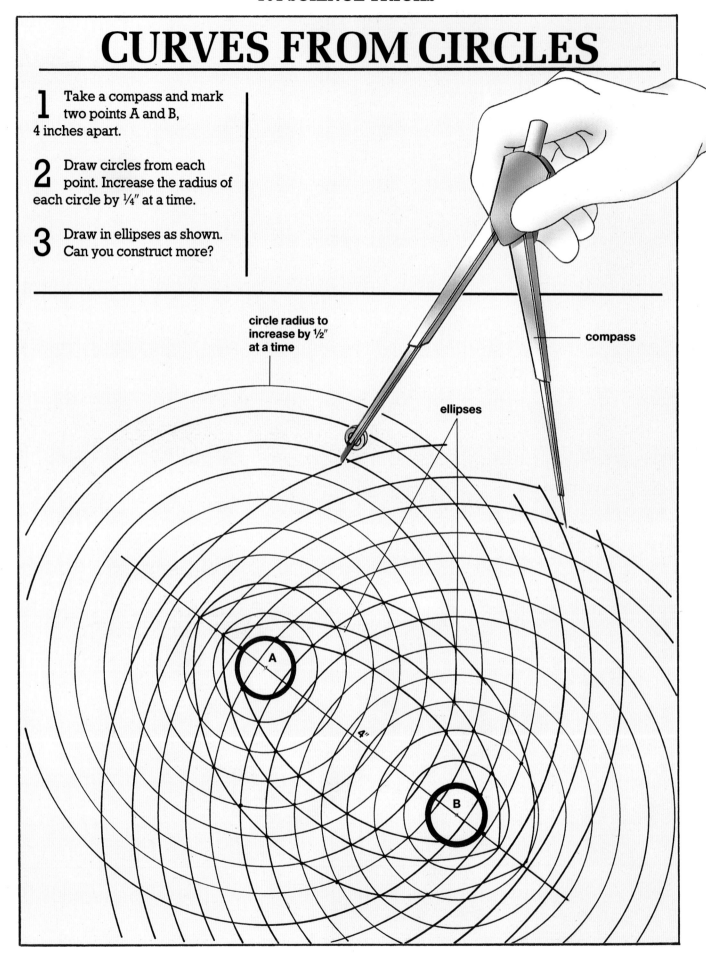

circle radius to increase by ½″ at a time

compass

ellipses

A

B

4″

You can make all sorts of patterns. Here are two examples. The patterns show the ellipses.

Try making other patterns by using different colors and choosing other parts of the design to color in.

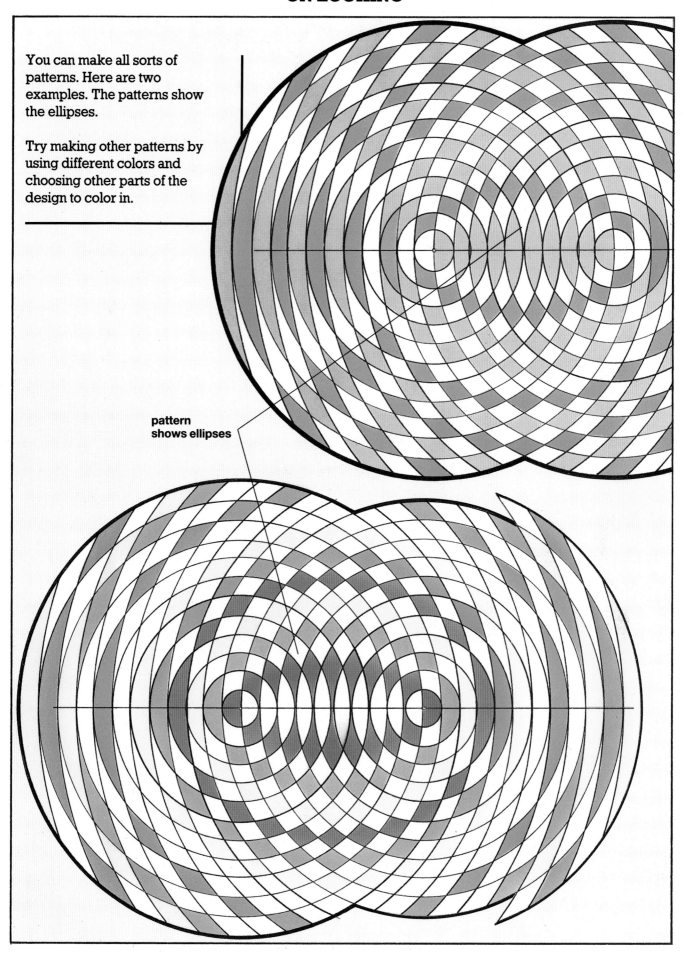

pattern
shows ellipses

CIRCLES FROM LINES

1 Take a compass again and draw a circle. Mark every 10 degrees around the circle using a protractor. You will end up with 36 marks.

2 Draw a line across the circle connecting two marks, A B. Take the next set of marks, C D, and connect them. Notice C is below A and D is above B. Repeat the pattern all round the circle.

You will find that you make a new circle at the center using your straight lines.

3 Draw a new line closer to the center E F. Draw the next line G H, again with G below E and H above F. Continue as before.

You will now make a new circle at the center.

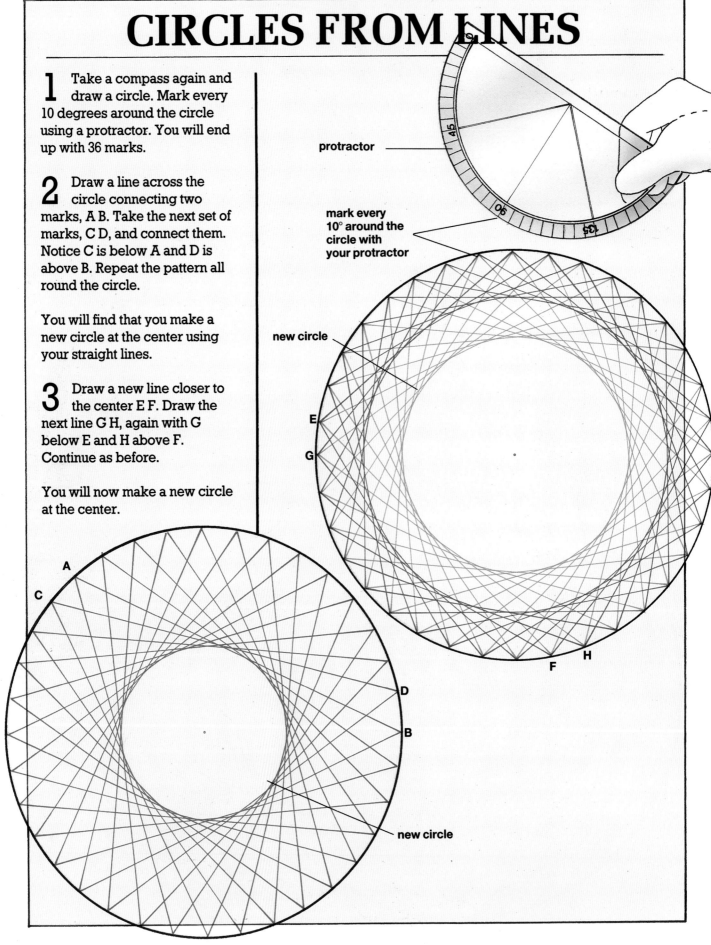

protractor

mark every 10° around the circle with your protractor

new circle

new circle

4 Draw a circle. Mark every 15 degrees around the circle using a protractor. You will end up with 24 marks. From every mark around the circle draw straight lines to every other mark. You will make the pattern below. It contains lots of new circles made from straight lines.

mark every 15°
around the circle
with your protractor

from every mark
draw straight
lines to every
other mark

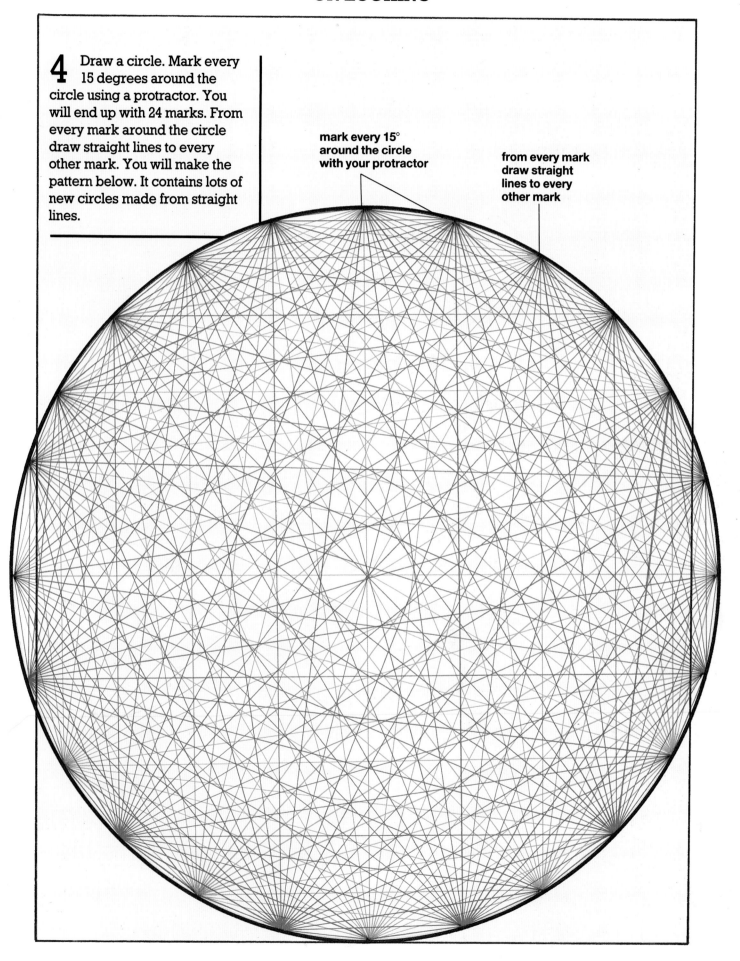

MORE CURVES

A SINGLE CURVE

1 Draw an angle ABC. Mark off ¼″ sections on each line.

2 Draw lines DH, EI, FJ, GK and so on. You will find that you make a curve.

Try longer lines. Try changing the size of the angle.

A DOUBLE CURVE

Draw a circle. Use a protractor to mark every 5 degrees. You should have 72 marks. Draw lines AB, BD, CF, DH, EJ, and so on. Each line drawn is one mark beyond the previous starting mark and two marks on from the previous ending mark.

The result is a double curve.

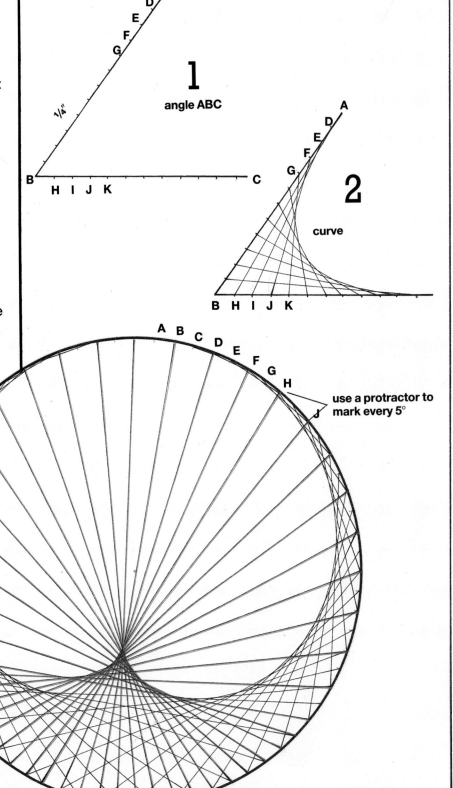

1 angle ABC

2 curve

double curve

use a protractor to mark every 5°

A NUMBER OF CURVES

Use a protractor to draw five angles of 72 degrees around the circle.

Mark off ¼″ sections on each line. Draw lines between the marks just as you did for the single curve on the previous page.

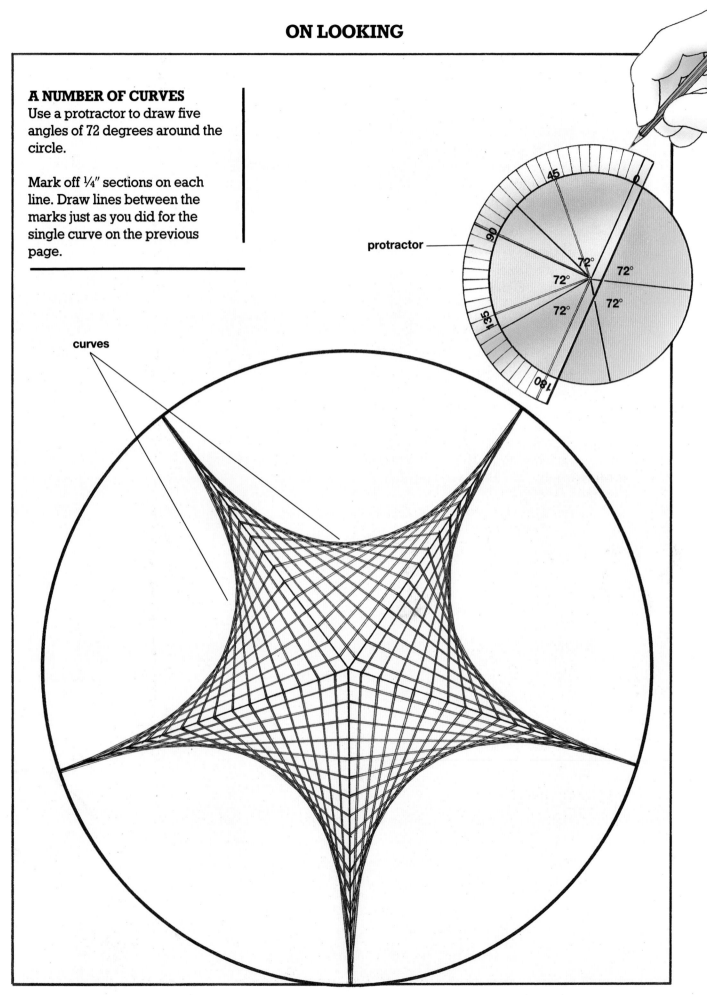

protractor

curves

CURVE STITCHING

With a darning needle and some yarn, you can create designs on cardboard using many of the curved patterns you learned to draw on the previous pages.

Draw an 8″ square on an 8½″ square piece of heavy cardboard. Mark off every ½″ around the square and punch out holes at your mark. Or use an 8½″ square of plywood with nails hammered partway in.

Connect the holes or nails to make a single curve at each corner.

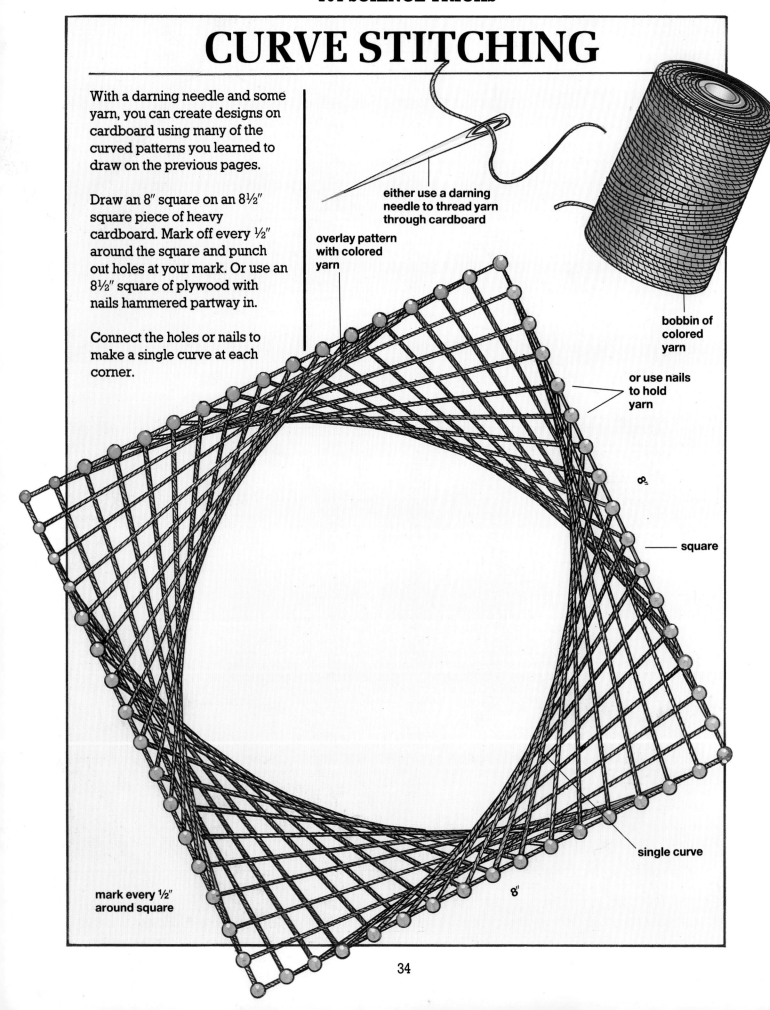

either use a darning needle to thread yarn through cardboard

overlay pattern with colored yarn

bobbin of colored yarn

or use nails to hold yarn

8″

square

8″

single curve

mark every ½″ around square

8″

SPIRAL

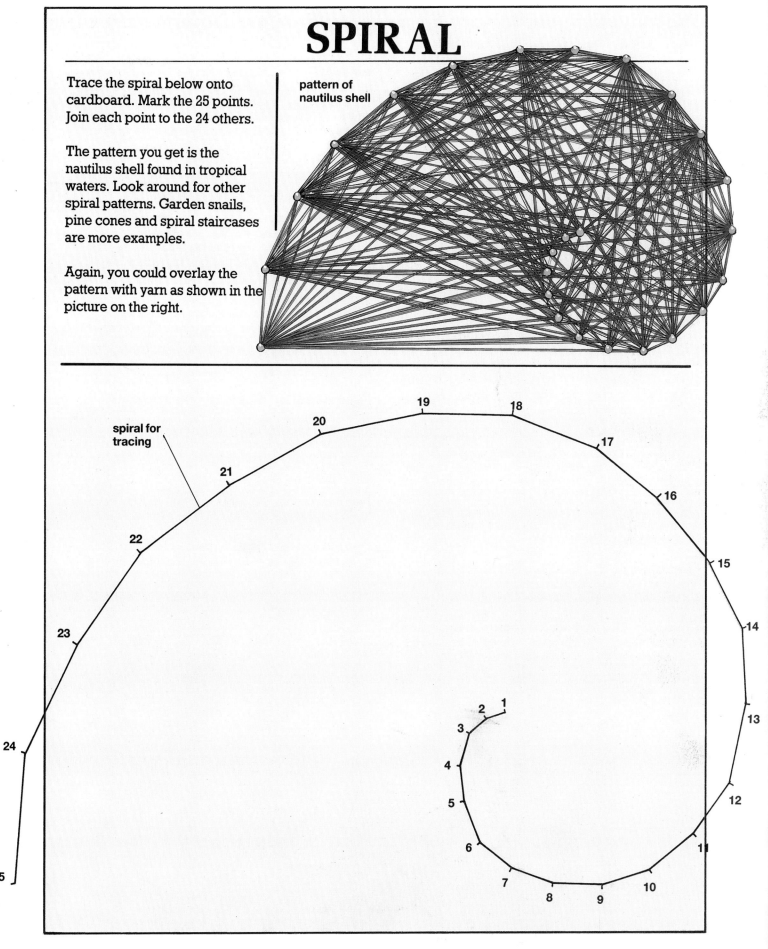

Trace the spiral below onto cardboard. Mark the 25 points. Join each point to the 24 others.

The pattern you get is the nautilus shell found in tropical waters. Look around for other spiral patterns. Garden snails, pine cones and spiral staircases are more examples.

Again, you could overlay the pattern with yarn as shown in the picture on the right.

pattern of nautilus shell

spiral for tracing

NOTES FOR PARENTS AND TEACHERS

Pages 7 – 27   These pages are concerned in some way or other with light and with the way we perceive things.

Children are learning that:
- light travels in straight lines
- light can be made to change direction
- shiny surfaces form images
- light can be reflected
- the brain can retain images to create an impression of movement.

All of these concepts are developed by carrying out the simple activities suggested. There is much that children can learn from investigations with mirrors.

Pages 7, 8 and 9   These are concerned with the way shiny mirror surfaces reflect well, and with reflective symmetry. They show how mirror images can be completed in both a horizontal and a vertical plane.

Pages 10 and 11   These show how putting two or more mirrors together can multiply the reflections and create a "kaleidoscopic" effect.

Pages 12 and 13   These show how light can be bent through an angle of 90 degrees using a mirror and how this effect is put into use to produce a periscope.

Pages 14 and 15   Carrying out the activities on Page 14 results in each eye receiving a separate image. The brain merges these together so that we see one composite picture. Page 11 illustrates how visual images can deceive.

Pages 16 and 17   The brain can retain images for a short while. This ability is made use of in the spinning picture toy called the thaumatrope.

Pages 18 – 21   Again the ability of the brain to retain images for a short while is made use of in the phenakistoscope to give an impression of continuous movement.

Pages 22 – 23   The flick book reinforces the way we retain images, as we see a rapidly moving succession of pictures. This creates the illusion of movement.

Pages 24 – 27   This section completes the work on light and optical toys by showing how to make a zoetrope. The retention of images by the brain is made use of in a toy that was a precursor of modern movies.

Pages 28 – 35   Here seeing is believing. We can use straight lines and circles to produce curves. This section is concerned with mathematical exploration. Children are learning that mathematics has patterns which is probably one of the most important things about it.

They are learning that:
- straight lines can be used to produce circles
- chords drawn to a circle produce an inner circle called an envelope
- there are ellipses
- there are patterns in mathematics.

Pages 28 and 29   Introduces children to ellipses and pattern-making.

Pages 30 and 31   Shows how drawing chords to a circle produces an inner circle that mathematicians call an envelope.

Pages 32 and 33   Develops the idea of getting curves from straight lines.

Pages 34 and 35   Shows how yarn can be used to make a picture commonly known as curved stitching. On Page 35 children find out how straight lines can be used to develop a spiral.

2
on the
Move

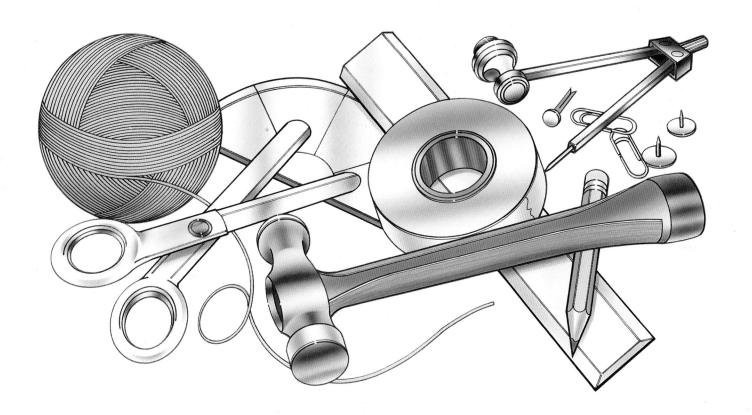

INTRODUCTION

Have you ever wondered what makes things move? What got the first boats, planes, rockets, and tanks going? In **On the Move** you will find lots of things to do and make. They will take you up in the air, along the ground and into the water and will enable you to see what makes things move. With a flick of the wrist your acrobatic plane will loop the loop. With a bit of wind your kite will take to the skies. With a few winds of the rubber band your spool tank will crawl and your water-screw boat will speed.

Find out how to make a paper windmill, a jumping Jack or a trotting mouse to give to your friends. Discover how to fling a boomerang, twirl a helicopter and spin a top. Some of the projects in **On the Move** may require the use of saws, drills or other tools. You'll find help in using tools safely on page 101 and you may need a parent or teacher to help you on some projects.

PAPER PLANE

Take a sheet of paper about 8½″ × 12″.

1 Fold the two opposite corners together.

2 Fold the bottom edge up half the distance of "x".

3 Fold the paper in half along the dotted line.

4 Fold the bottom sections upward along the dotted line.

5 Fold the wings down along the dotted line.

6 Staple the nose and tail.

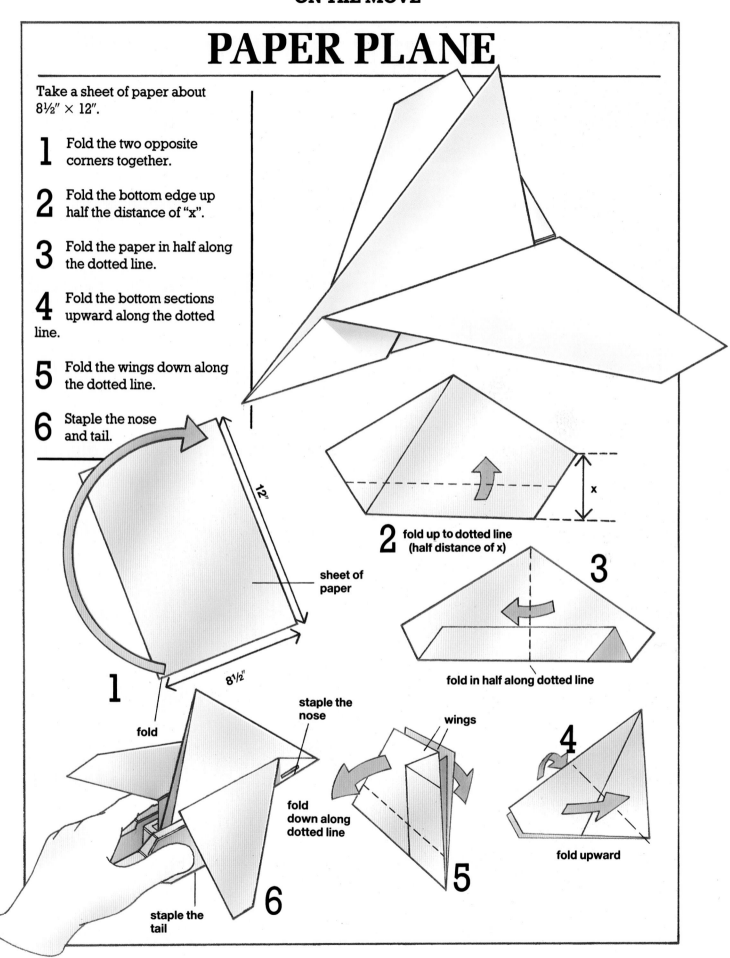

1 12″ 8½″ sheet of paper fold

2 fold up to dotted line (half distance of x) x

3 fold in half along dotted line

4 fold upward

5 wings fold down along dotted line

6 staple the nose staple the tail

PAPER DART

Use one sheet of paper (8½" × 12") to make a paper dart.

1 Fold in half.

2 Open out and fold the corner to the center.

3 Fold the other corner to the center.

4 Fold the new corners as shown.

5 It should look like this.

6 Turn the sheet over.

7 Fold one side to center.

8 Fold the other.

9 Fold in half. Fold down wings as shown.

10 Hold the center fold and open.

11 Fasten the paper dart with tape.

12 Launch it.

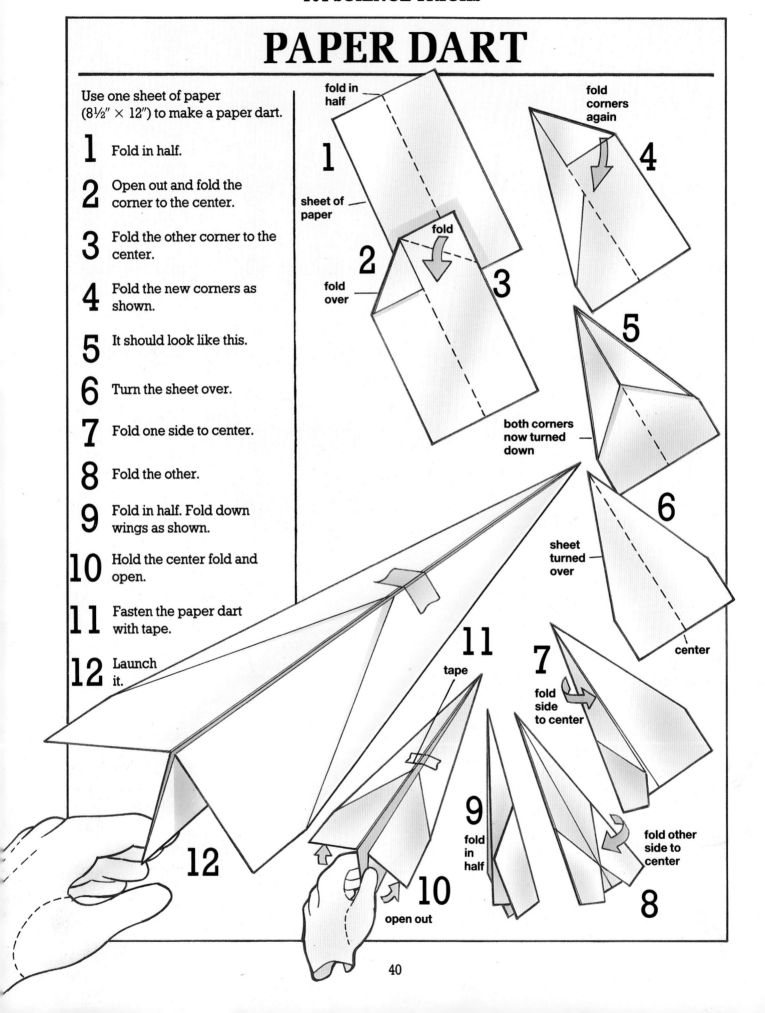

1 fold in half — sheet of paper

2 fold over — fold

3

4 fold corners again

5 both corners now turned down

6 sheet turned over — center

7 fold side to center

8 fold other side to center

9 fold in half

10 open out

11 tape

12

40

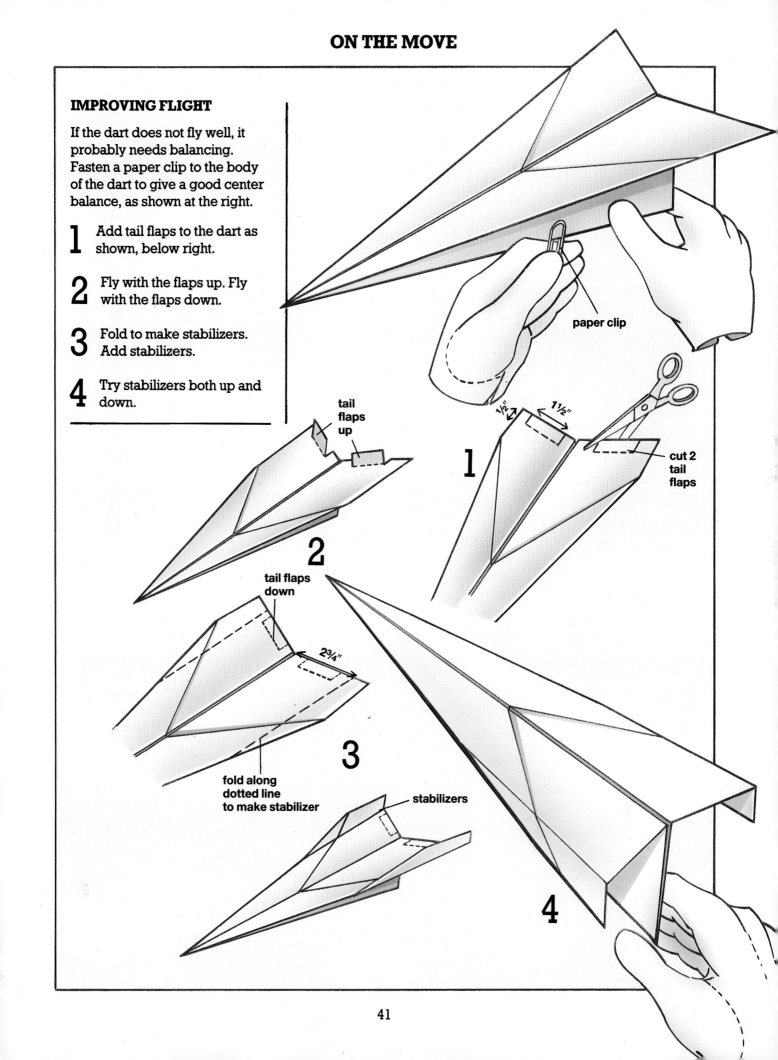

IMPROVING FLIGHT

If the dart does not fly well, it probably needs balancing. Fasten a paper clip to the body of the dart to give a good center balance, as shown at the right.

1 Add tail flaps to the dart as shown, below right.

2 Fly with the flaps up. Fly with the flaps down.

3 Fold to make stabilizers. Add stabilizers.

4 Try stabilizers both up and down.

paper clip

1

½" 1½"

cut 2 tail flaps

tail flaps up

2

tail flaps down

2¾"

3

fold along dotted line to make stabilizer

stabilizers

4

DELTA WING

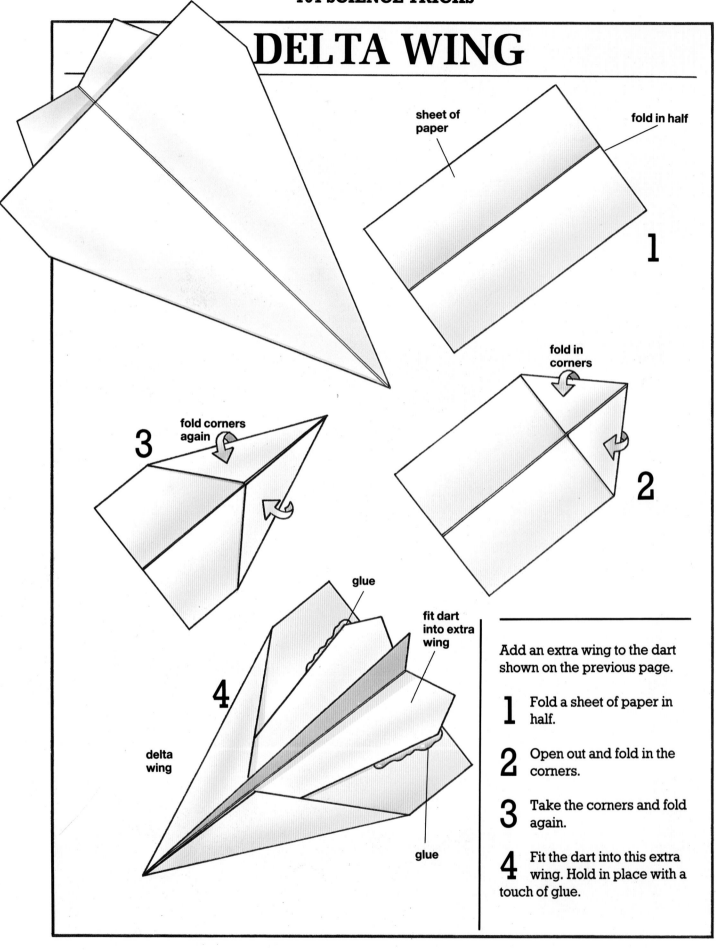

sheet of paper

fold in half

1

fold in corners

2

fold corners again

3

glue

fit dart into extra wing

4

delta wing

glue

Add an extra wing to the dart shown on the previous page.

1 Fold a sheet of paper in half.

2 Open out and fold in the corners.

3 Take the corners and fold again.

4 Fit the dart into this extra wing. Hold in place with a touch of glue.

ACROBATIC PLANE

1 Fold a sheet of notebook paper crosswise.

2 Open up and fold a crease ½″ from the edge of the long side.

3 Fold and fold again several times.

4 Refold at center line. Cut out a notch in the paper as shown.

5 Open out the acrobatic plane.

6 Fold the wing tips of the plane up.

7 Fold down the outer edges of the tail.

8 Check the plane for symmetry. It is essential that one half is a mirror image of the other.

9 Launch the plane gently away from you with a slight downward motion.

TIPS

1 If the plane glides all right but moves from side to side, check the symmetry again.

2 If the plane dives, turn the trailing edge of the tail up a little.

3 If the plane moves in a wave-like motion, turn the trailing edges of the tail down. If this is not successful, the plane may be too heavy in the tail. Try a tiny piece of clay or a paper clip on the nose.

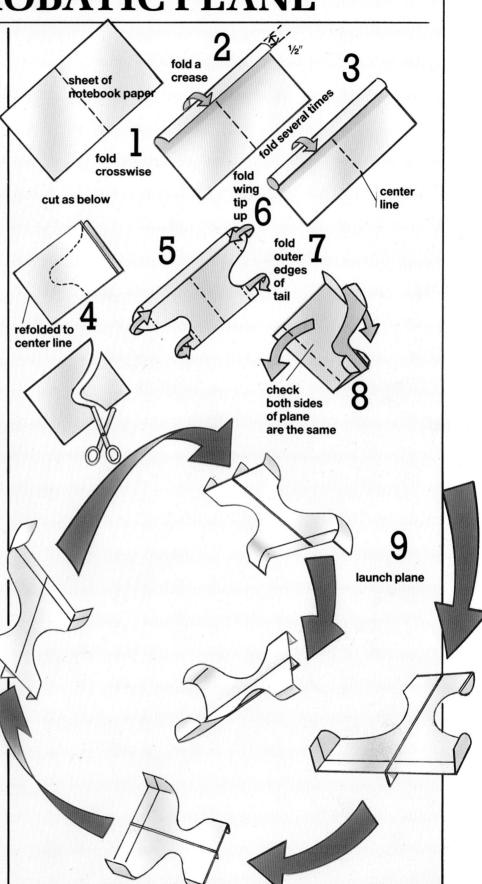

1 sheet of notebook paper
fold crosswise
cut as below

2 fold a crease ½″
fold wing tip up
fold several times
center line

3

4 refolded to center line

5

6

7 fold outer edges of tail

8 check both sides of plane are the same

9 launch plane

43

BALSA WOOD GLIDER

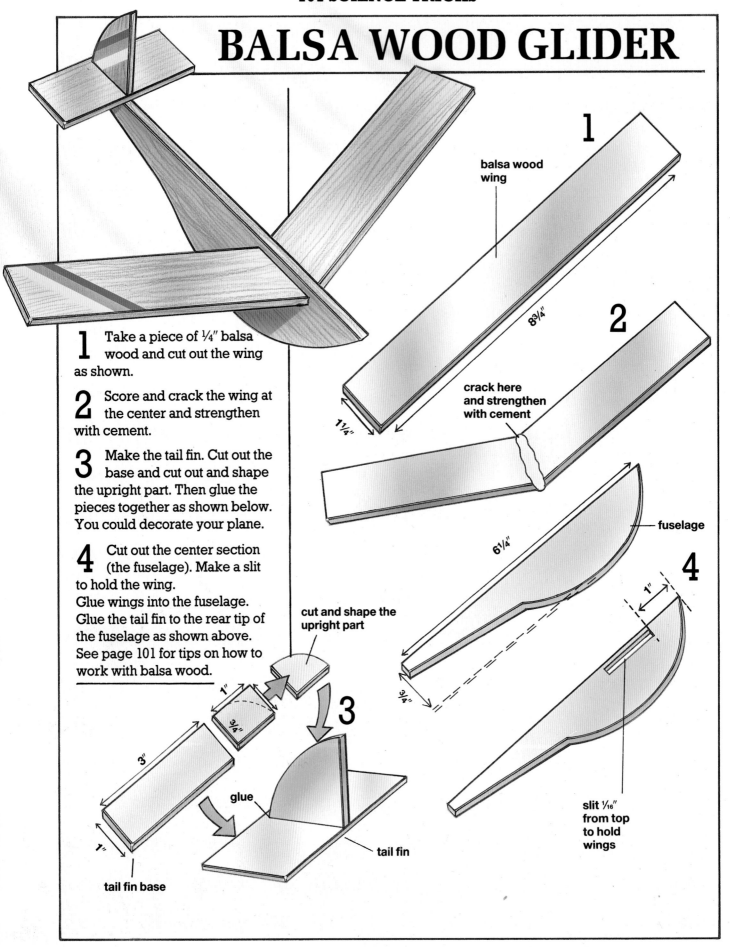

1 Take a piece of ¼″ balsa wood and cut out the wing as shown.

2 Score and crack the wing at the center and strengthen with cement.

3 Make the tail fin. Cut out the base and cut out and shape the upright part. Then glue the pieces together as shown below. You could decorate your plane.

4 Cut out the center section (the fuselage). Make a slit to hold the wing.
Glue wings into the fuselage. Glue the tail fin to the rear tip of the fuselage as shown above. See page 101 for tips on how to work with balsa wood.

balsa wood wing

8¾″

1¼″

crack here and strengthen with cement

fuselage

6¼″

¾″

1″

cut and shape the upright part

1″

¾″

3″

1″

glue

tail fin

tail fin base

slit ¹⁄₁₆″ from top to hold wings

JET ROCKET

This balloon rocket runs on nylon fishing line fastened tightly across a room.

1 Thread two short pieces of drinking straw onto the line.

2 Blow up the balloon. Close the neck of the balloon with a metal clip.

3 Tape the straws to the inflated balloon. Make sure the fishing line is taut and straight.

4 When you are ready to launch your rocket, remove the clip to release the balloon.

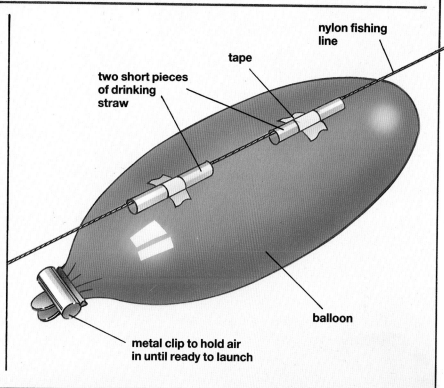

nylon fishing line

tape

two short pieces of drinking straw

balloon

metal clip to hold air in until ready to launch

PROPELLER-DRIVEN PLANE

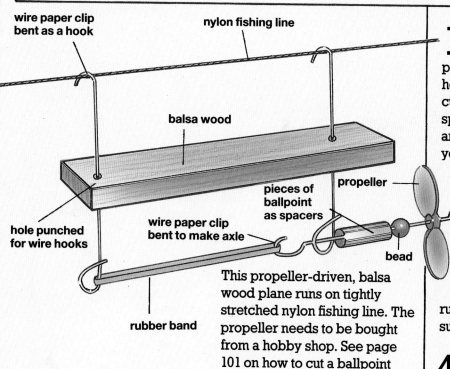

wire paper clip bent as a hook

nylon fishing line

balsa wood

hole punched for wire hooks

wire paper clip bent to make axle

pieces of ballpoint as spacers

propeller

bead

rubber band

1 Use a wire paper clip to make the axle to hold the propeller. You need a bead to help it run smoothly and a piece cut off an old ballpoint as a spacer. Thread the piece of pen and the bead and propeller onto your wire axle as shown.

2 Bend two other paper clips to make the wire hooks that pass through the balsa wood body of the plane.

3 Wind the propeller around and around to twist the rubber band and give the plane super energy.

4 Release the propeller and watch the plane whizz along.

This propeller-driven, balsa wood plane runs on tightly stretched nylon fishing line. The propeller needs to be bought from a hobby shop. See page 101 on how to cut a ballpoint pen.

PARACHUTES

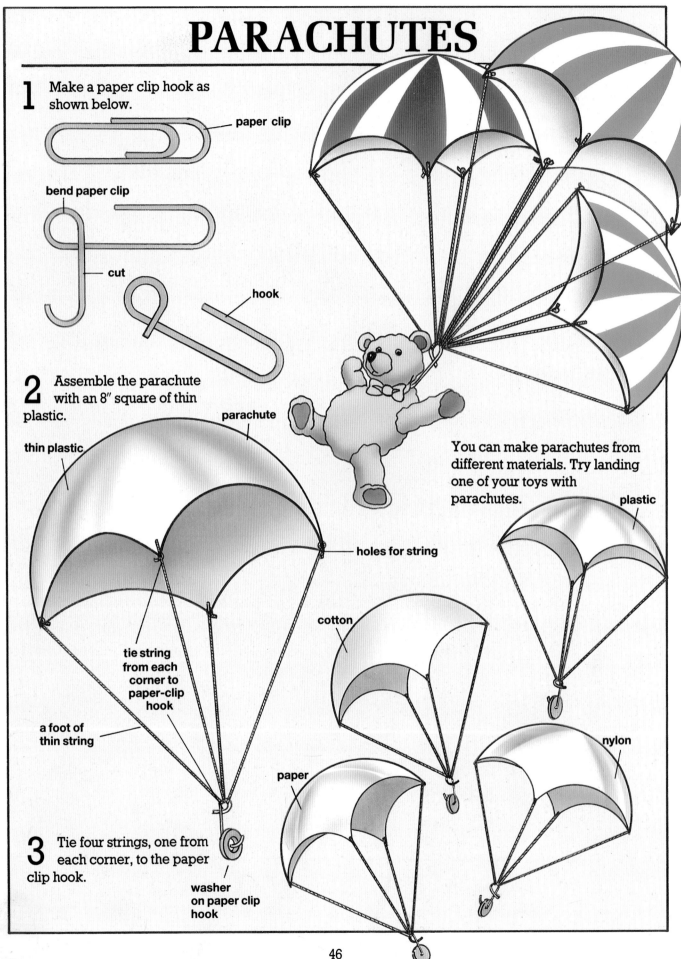

1 Make a paper clip hook as shown below.

paper clip

bend paper clip

cut

hook

2 Assemble the parachute with an 8″ square of thin plastic.

parachute

thin plastic

holes for string

tie string from each corner to paper-clip hook

a foot of thin string

3 Tie four strings, one from each corner, to the paper clip hook.

washer on paper clip hook

You can make parachutes from different materials. Try landing one of your toys with parachutes.

plastic

cotton

nylon

paper

PAPER SPINNERS

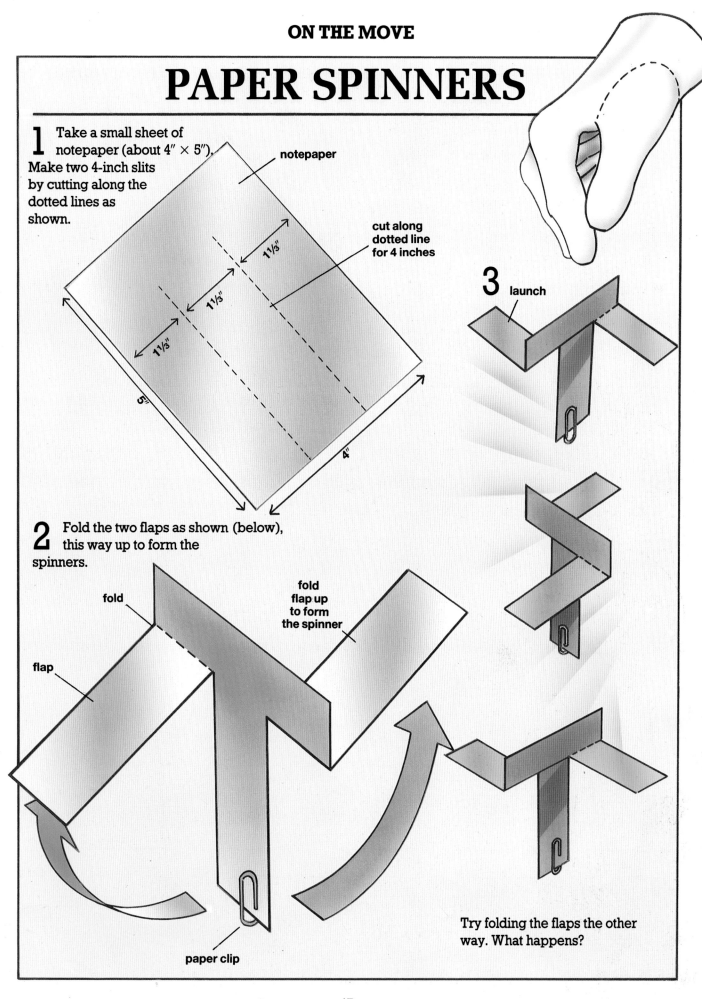

1 Take a small sheet of notepaper (about 4″ × 5″). Make two 4-inch slits by cutting along the dotted lines as shown.

notepaper

cut along dotted line for 4 inches

1⅓″ 1⅓″ 1⅓″ 1⅓″

5″

4″

3 launch

2 Fold the two flaps as shown (below), this way up to form the spinners.

fold

flap

fold flap up to form the spinner

paper clip

Try folding the flaps the other way. What happens?

47

BOOMERANGS

1 Trace the outline of this boomerang onto light cardboard. Cut it out.

2 Bend the tip AB slightly.

3 Flick the boomerang from the back of a book. You will need to experiment with the angle you hold the book.

Keep trying!

If the bend in the tip is slight, the boomerang will fly in a large orbit. If the bend is more pronounced, the boomerang will have a smaller flying circle.

4 The Y shape does not look like a boomerang. However, it is just as effective. Trace the outline. Cut it out.

5 Flick the Y shape from the back of a book. Again you will need to experiment with the angle of launch. Practice makes perfect!

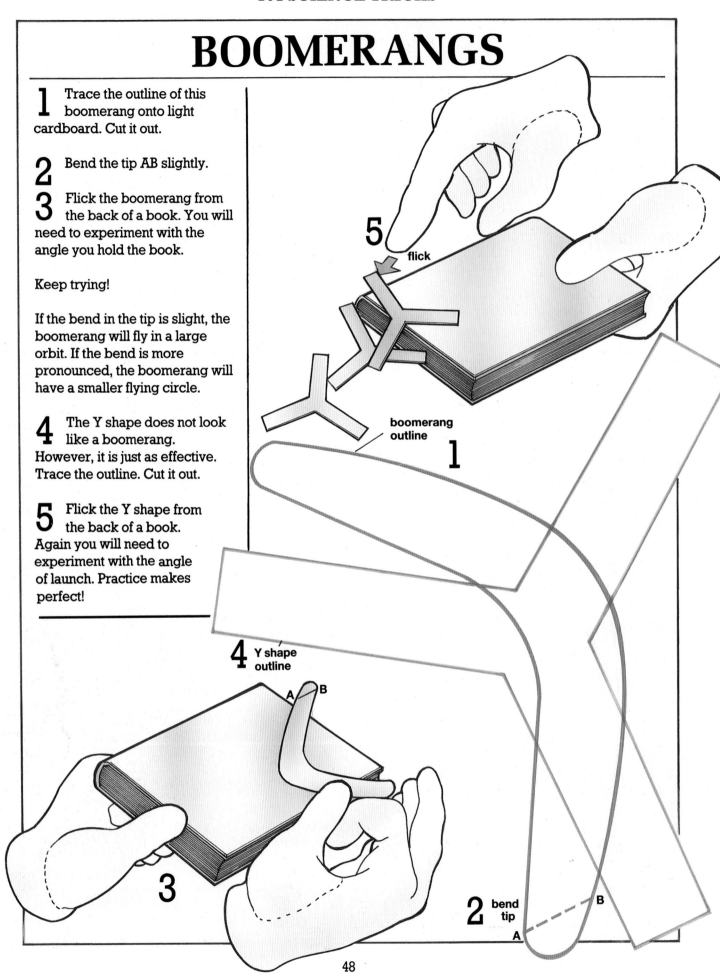

5 flick

1 boomerang outline

4 Y shape outline

3

2 bend tip

A B

48

WINDMILLS

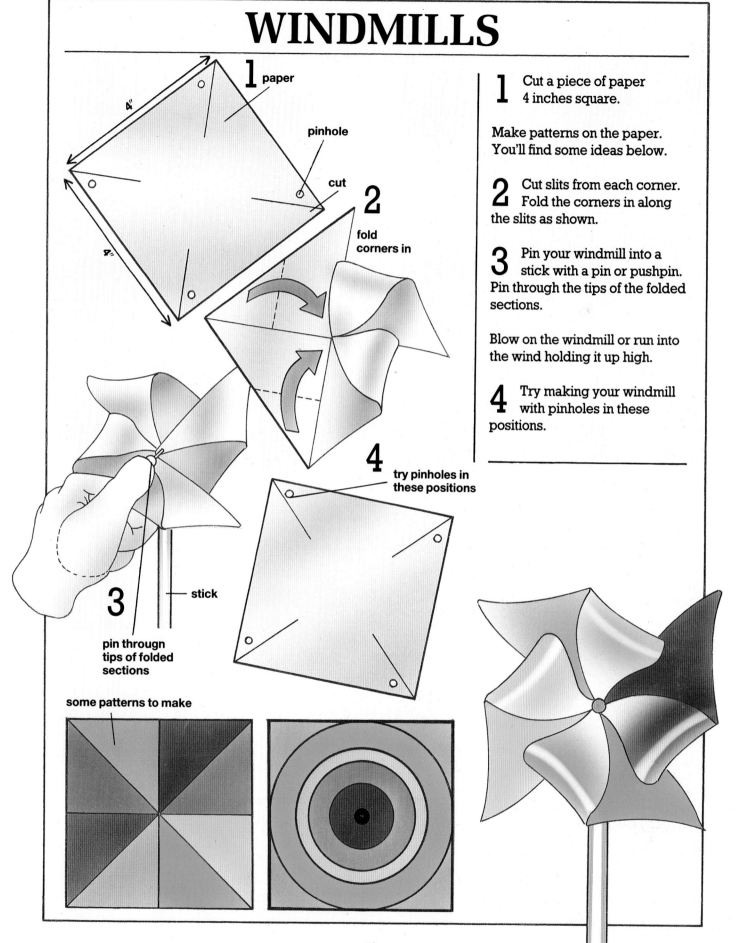

1 paper

pinhole

cut

2

fold corners in

3

stick

pin through tips of folded sections

4

try pinholes in these positions

some patterns to make

1 Cut a piece of paper 4 inches square.

Make patterns on the paper. You'll find some ideas below.

2 Cut slits from each corner. Fold the corners in along the slits as shown.

3 Pin your windmill into a stick with a pin or pushpin. Pin through the tips of the folded sections.

Blow on the windmill or run into the wind holding it up high.

4 Try making your windmill with pinholes in these positions.

TIN HELICOPTER

THINGS TO COLLECT

pencil

nails

tin cutters

pliers

string

tin box

hammer

wooden spool

tape

1 cut off nail tops

thread spool

cover tin with tape for safety

make holes in tin shape

same space as between nails

2 tape

pencil

3

4 twist

5 propeller sits on nails

This project calls for tin snips and an electric drill. See page 101 for notes on safe tool use.

1 Hammer the nails into the cotton reel. Cut off their tops with the pliers.

2 Wind the tape round and round the pencil, enough for the spool to sit on.

3 Rest a small piece of tin on top of the nails sticking out of the spool and tap it lightly with a hammer to mark where you want to drill. Clamp the tin securely, with scrap wood under it, and drill two holes at your marks. Cut out the propeller shape shown above. Be sure to keep the holes in the centers of the blades. Cover the propeller with tape.

4 Twist the tin shape to make your propeller.

5 Sit the propeller on the nails.

Take great care. Hold the helicopter well above your head and well away from people.

6 Wrap string round and round the spool. Sit the spool on the pencil. Pull the string sharply to spin the propeller and set the helicopter spinning upward.

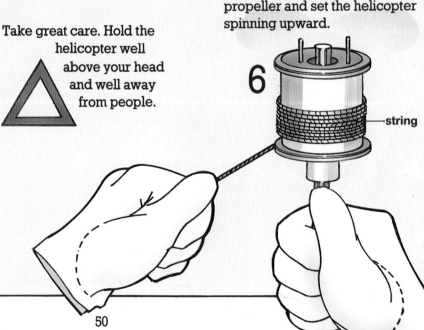

6

string

PLASTIC HELICOPTER

Take any flat-sided plastic container.

1 Use a pair of scissors to cut a strip of plastic from this container.

2 Make a hole through the center of the plastic strip with a nail.

3 Push a pencil through the plastic. Twist the plastic strip slightly to make your helicopter.

4 Spin the helicopter in your hand and throw it into the air.

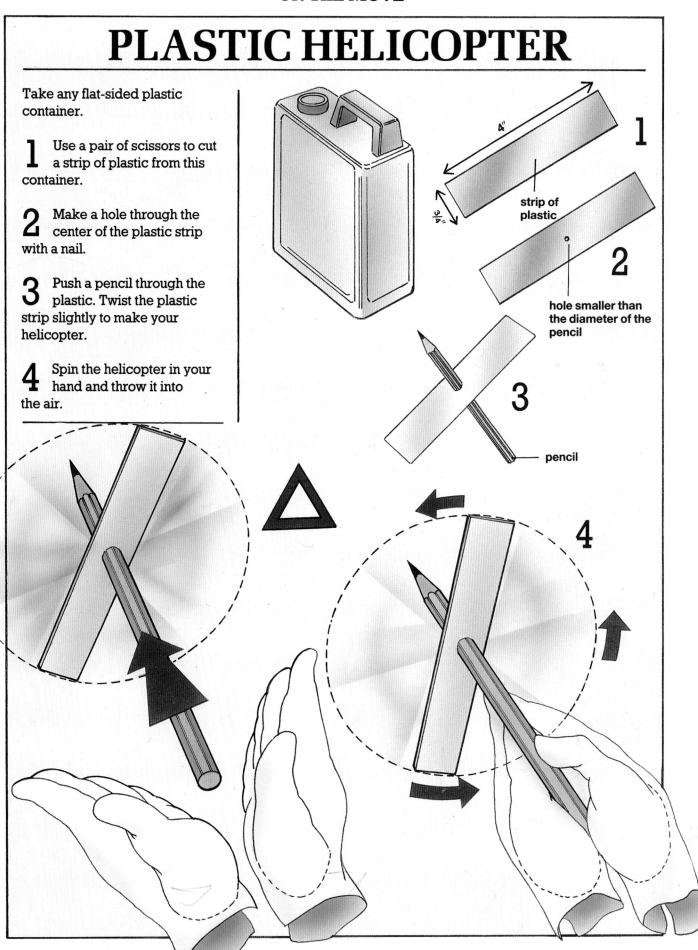

4"

¾"

strip of plastic

1

2

hole smaller than the diameter of the pencil

3

pencil

4

KITE

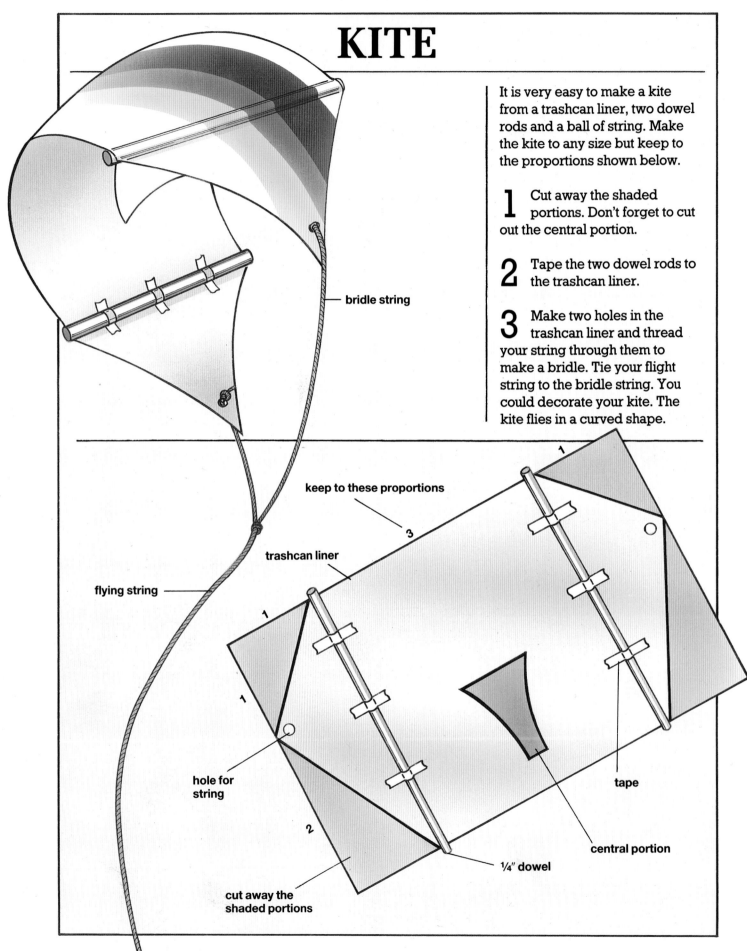

It is very easy to make a kite from a trashcan liner, two dowel rods and a ball of string. Make the kite to any size but keep to the proportions shown below.

1 Cut away the shaded portions. Don't forget to cut out the central portion.

2 Tape the two dowel rods to the trashcan liner.

3 Make two holes in the trashcan liner and thread your string through them to make a bridle. Tie your flight string to the bridle string. You could decorate your kite. The kite flies in a curved shape.

bridle string

keep to these proportions

trashcan liner

flying string

hole for string

cut away the shaded portions

¼" dowel

central portion

tape

HOT-AIR BALLOON

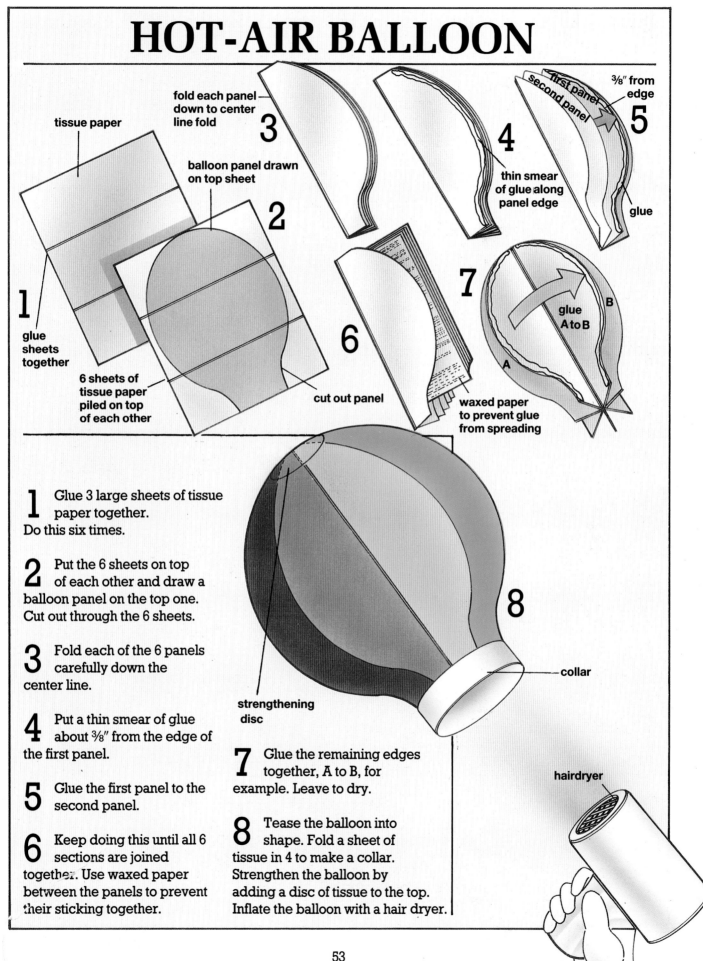

tissue paper

fold each panel down to center line fold

3

balloon panel drawn on top sheet

2

4

thin smear of glue along panel edge

5

³⁄₈″ from edge

first panel

second panel

glue

1

glue sheets together

6 sheets of tissue paper piled on top of each other

6

cut out panel

7

glue A to B

B

A

waxed paper to prevent glue from spreading

strengthening disc

8

collar

hairdryer

1 Glue 3 large sheets of tissue paper together. Do this six times.

2 Put the 6 sheets on top of each other and draw a balloon panel on the top one. Cut out through the 6 sheets.

3 Fold each of the 6 panels carefully down the center line.

4 Put a thin smear of glue about ³⁄₈″ from the edge of the first panel.

5 Glue the first panel to the second panel.

6 Keep doing this until all 6 sections are joined together. Use waxed paper between the panels to prevent their sticking together.

7 Glue the remaining edges together, A to B, for example. Leave to dry.

8 Tease the balloon into shape. Fold a sheet of tissue in 4 to make a collar. Strengthen the balloon by adding a disc of tissue to the top. Inflate the balloon with a hair dryer.

SPOOL TANK

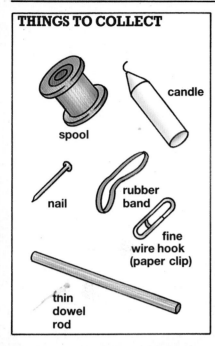

THINGS TO COLLECT

spool

candle

nail

rubber band

fine wire hook (paper clip)

thin dowel rod

1 Cut a ½″ piece off the candle. See page 101 for help on cutting the candle.

2 Make a hole through the center of the candle by pulling out the wick. Thread the rubber band through the candle and secure it with the dowel.

3 Pull the free end of the rubber band through the spool with the wire hook.

4 Secure the free end of the rubber band with a nail.

5 Wind the rubber band by twisting the dowel rod around and around. Place the spool tank on the ground and watch it move.

6 Wind the spool with a rubber band to help the tank grip when climbing slopes.

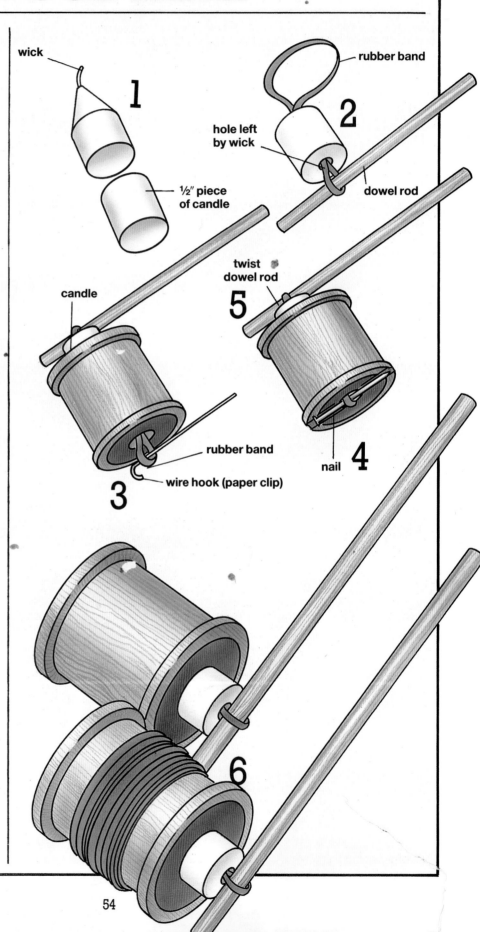

wick

1

½″ piece of candle

rubber band

2

hole left by wick

dowel rod

candle

3

rubber band

wire hook (paper clip)

twist dowel rod

5

4

nail

6

DRINK CAN DRAGSTER

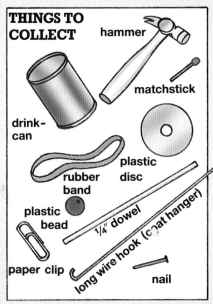

THINGS TO COLLECT

hammer

matchstick

drink-can

rubber band

plastic disc

plastic bead

¼" dowel

long wire hook (coat hanger)

paper clip

nail

1 Make a hole through the blank end of the can with a nail.

2 Straighten out the paper clip to make a hook.

3 Put the hook through the disc and the plastic bead.

4 Bend the straight end of the wire on the dowel rod and twist it around.

5 Use the long wire hook to pull a rubber band through the can.

6 Secure the other end of the rubber band to a matchstick.

7 Wind the rod around and around so that the rubber band winds tightly. Then release the dragster.

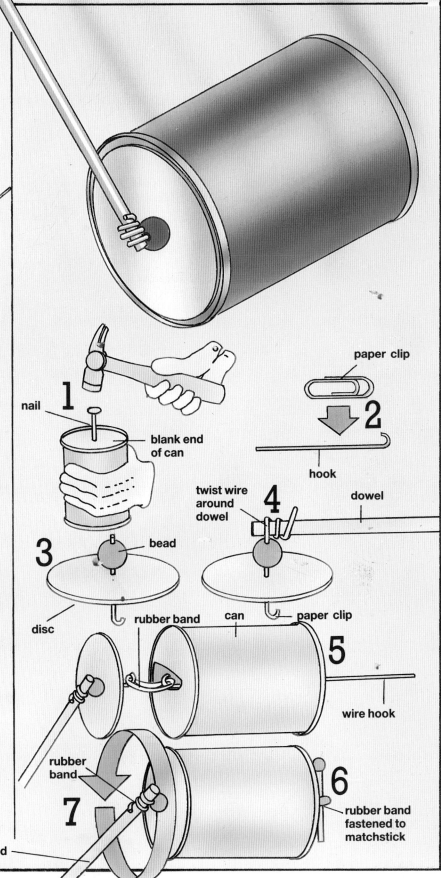

LAND YACHT

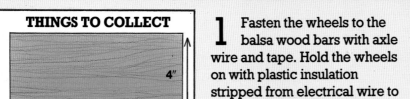

THINGS TO COLLECT

1/4" balsa sheet

4"

6½"

2 balsa wood bars

½"

½"

4 inches

4 model plane wheels

reel

peg

two thin dowel rods

plastic covered wire

tape

trashcan liner

1 Fasten the wheels to the balsa wood bars with axle wire and tape. Hold the wheels on with plastic insulation stripped from electrical wire to act as a stop.

2 Glue the balsa sheet to the balsa bars. Glue on the spool. Fix the dowel rod boom to the clothes peg with rubber

bands. Put the dowel rod mast into the center of the spool. Fix the boom to the mast with the clothes peg.

3 Cut and paste a piece of trashcan liner or other material as a sail. Decorate your sail. Try your land yacht on a hard flat surface when there is some wind.

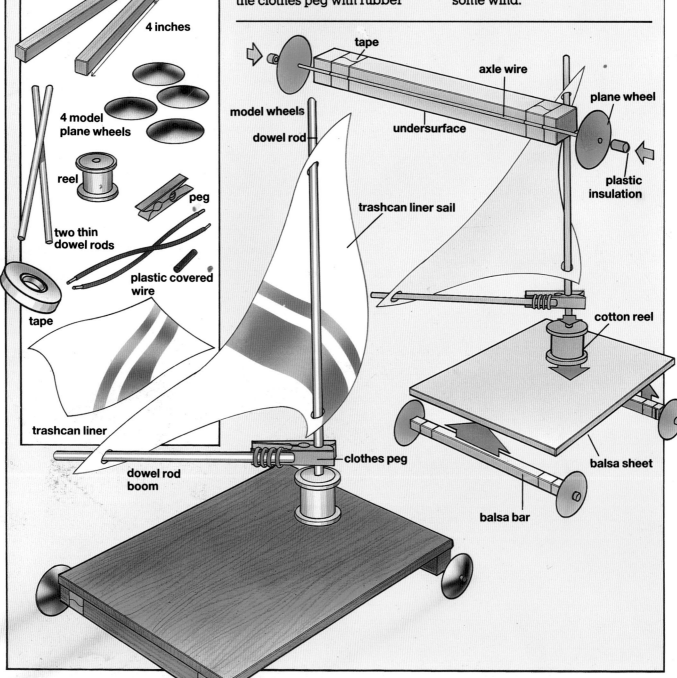

tape

axle wire

plane wheel

model wheels

dowel rod

undersurface

plastic insulation

trashcan liner sail

cotton reel

clothes peg

balsa sheet

dowel rod boom

balsa bar

TROLLEY

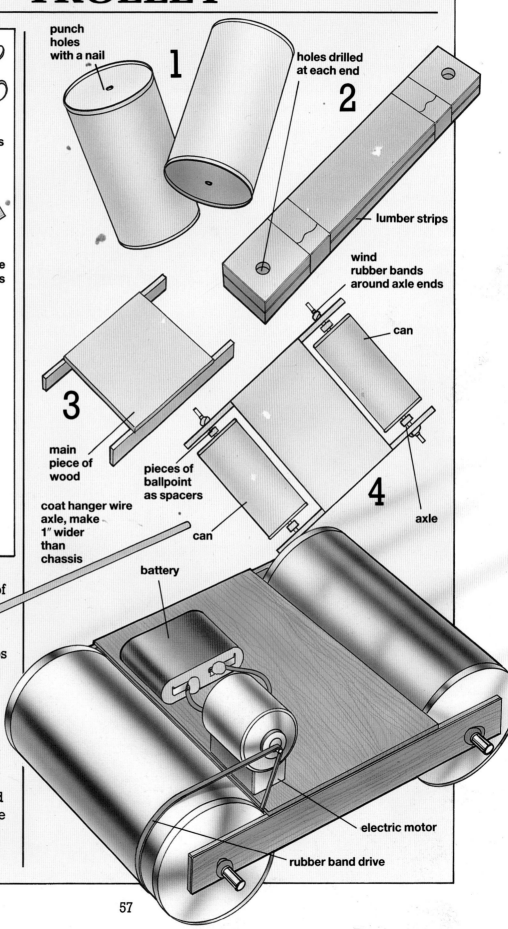

THINGS TO COLLECT

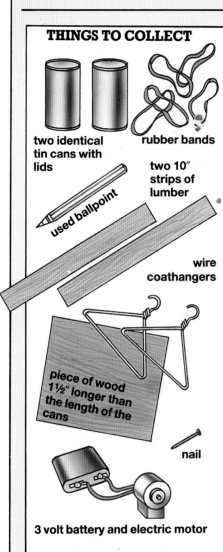

two identical tin cans with lids

rubber bands

used ballpoint

two 10″ strips of lumber

wire coathangers

piece of wood 1½″ longer than the length of the cans

nail

3 volt battery and electric motor

punch holes with a nail

holes drilled at each end

1

2

lumber strips

wind rubber bands around axle ends

can

3

main piece of wood

coat hanger wire axle, make 1″ wider than chassis

pieces of ballpoint as spacers

can

4

axle

battery

electric motor

rubber band drive

1 Make holes in the center of each end of your cans.

2 Drill holes at each end of timber strips (see page 101). Check with a parent or teacher first before you use the drill.

3 Glue and pin the strips to the main piece of timber.

4 Assemble using pieces of ballpoint as spacers. Wind a rubber band around each axle end to prevent it from slipping out. Fix the can to the motor using a rubber band.

JUMPING JACK

1 Trace these pieces of the Jack's body (below) onto cardboard. Cut them out and decorate them.

2 Fasten the arms and legs to the main body with paper fasteners. Make small holes in the arms, legs and main body and attach the string as shown.

3 Make a small hole in the Jack's head and attach the string to the head as shown. Hold the Jack by the string from the head. Pull the lower string to make him jump.

2

paper fasteners

small holes for string

3

string

1

arms

outline of main body

legs

cut shapes from card

MOUSE ON THE MOVE

1 Trace the legs and body of the mouse onto cardboard.

2 Cut the shapes out and color them in.

3 Fasten the legs to the mouse body with a paper fastener. Make sure the legs spin freely.

4 Fasten a balsa rod to the mouse with glue. Use it to nudge the mouse along.

5 Fasten a string to the mouse's bottom to make a tail.

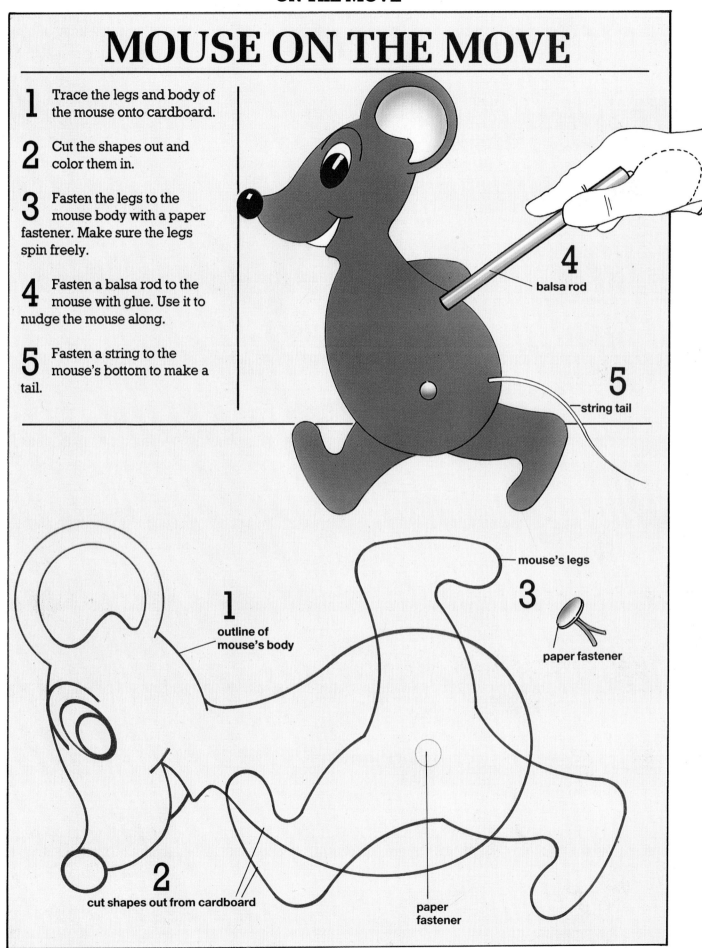

4 balsa rod

5 string tail

1 outline of mouse's body

2 cut shapes out from cardboard

3 mouse's legs

paper fastener

paper fastener

TOPS

Make some tops from cardboard.

1 With a compass draw some circles about 3 inches in diameter.

2 Decorate these circles. Make up different designs and colored patterns.

3 Cut out your colored circles. Push a piece of dowel rod or a pencil through the center of each circle to act as a spindle.

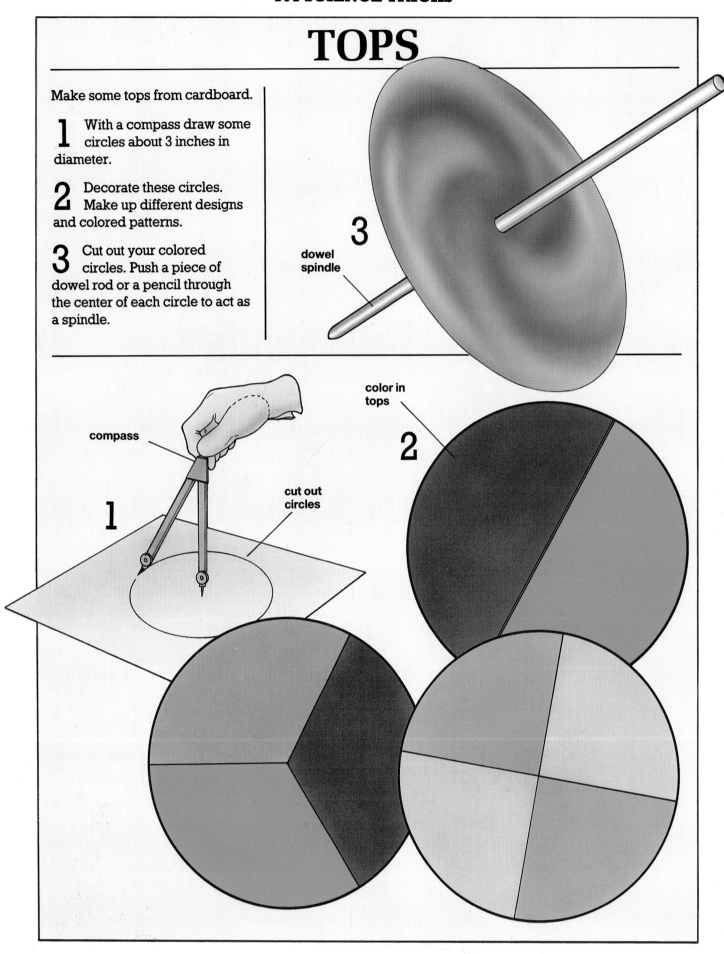

3

dowel spindle

compass

1

cut out circles

color in tops

2

DESIGNS AND PATTERNS

Try spinning your tops.
See what happens to
the colors and patterns
as they spin.

SPINNERS

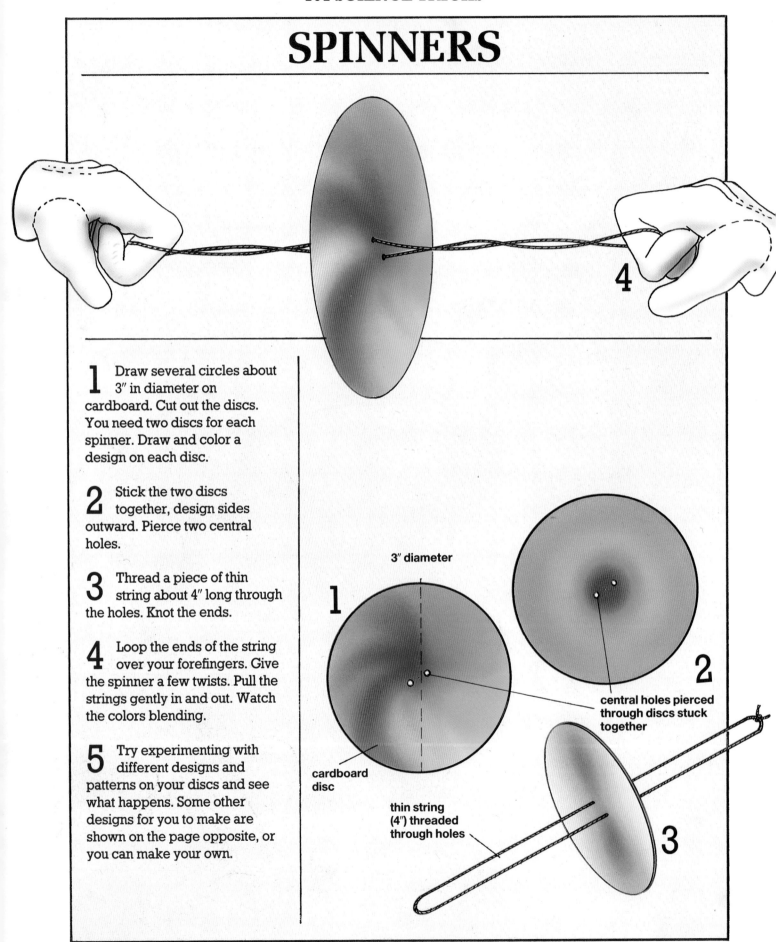

1 Draw several circles about 3″ in diameter on cardboard. Cut out the discs. You need two discs for each spinner. Draw and color a design on each disc.

2 Stick the two discs together, design sides outward. Pierce two central holes.

3 Thread a piece of thin string about 4″ long through the holes. Knot the ends.

4 Loop the ends of the string over your forefingers. Give the spinner a few twists. Pull the strings gently in and out. Watch the colors blending.

5 Try experimenting with different designs and patterns on your discs and see what happens. Some other designs for you to make are shown on the page opposite, or you can make your own.

3″ diameter

cardboard disc

central holes pierced through discs stuck together

thin string (4″) threaded through holes

MAKE OTHER DESIGNS

5

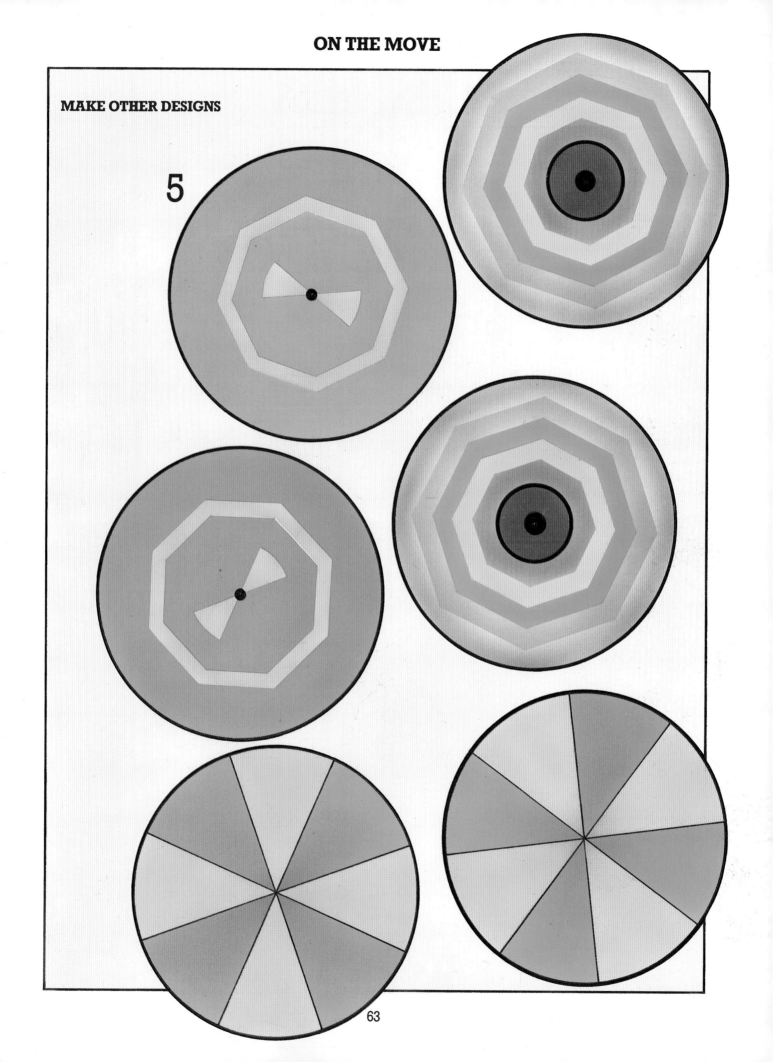

PAPER BOAT

1 Use a sheet of paper about 8″ square. Fold the sides to the middle.

2 Fold in the corners to the middle.

3 Make creases, as shown, and fold in.

4 Crease horizontally across, as shown, and fold in.

5 Open the boat and turn it inside out.

Float the boat along a stream or in the bathtub.

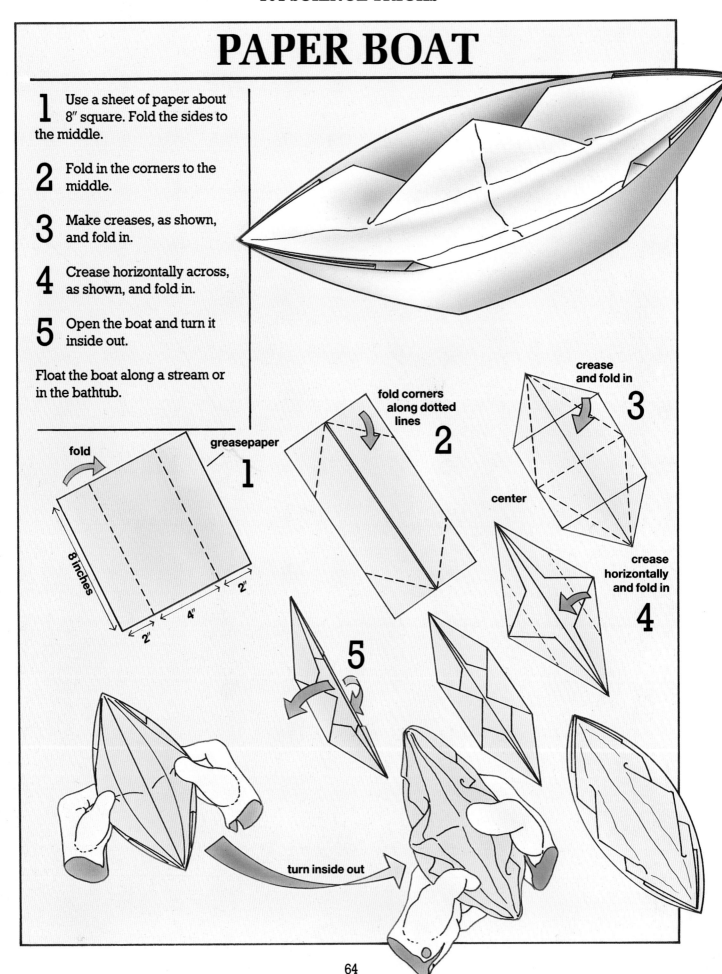

BALSA WOOD BOATS

1 You need some balsa wood to make the bases or "hulls" of your boats. Look at the different shaped hulls below and choose some shapes to try. Cut them out.

2 Make sails for your boats with knitting needles and paper. Look at the different shaped sails below and choose some shapes to try. Cut out the sails from paper and attach them to your hulls with knitting needles.

Small sails for small boats can be made from cocktail sticks and paper.

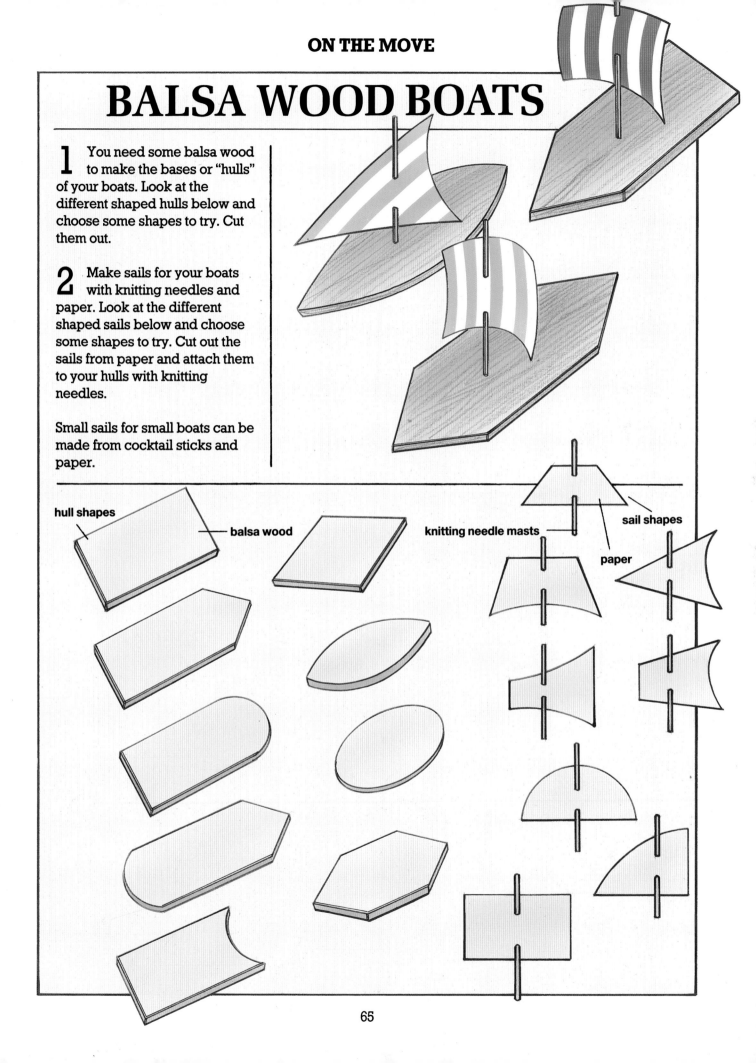

hull shapes

balsa wood

knitting needle masts

sail shapes

paper

POWER-DRIVEN BOATS

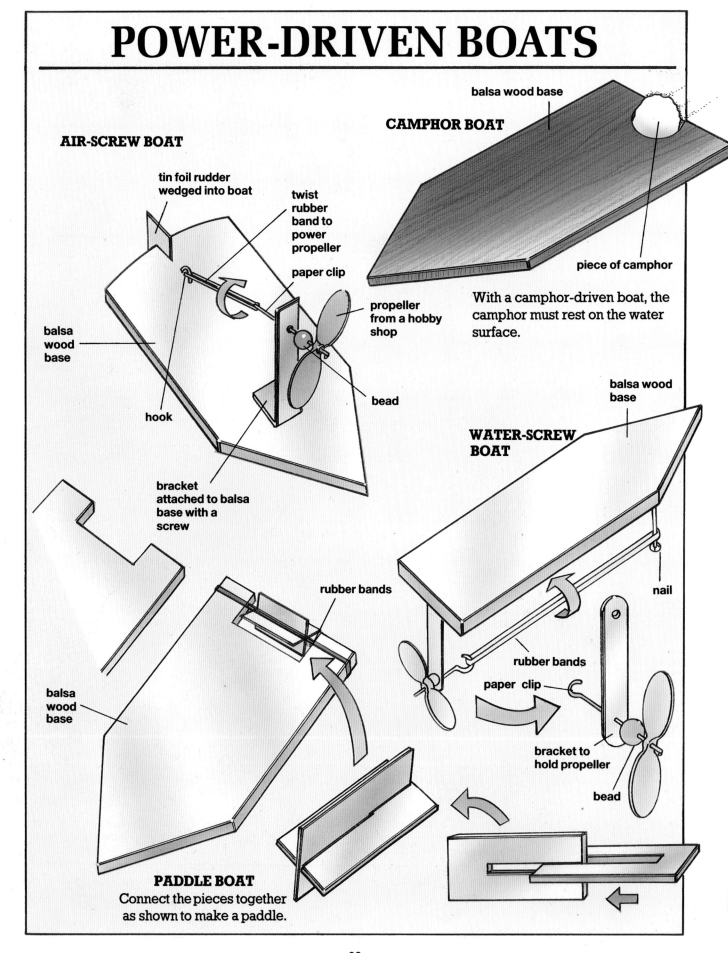

CAMPHOR BOAT

balsa wood base

piece of camphor

With a camphor-driven boat, the camphor must rest on the water surface.

AIR-SCREW BOAT

tin foil rudder wedged into boat

twist rubber band to power propeller

paper clip

propeller from a hobby shop

balsa wood base

bead

hook

bracket attached to balsa base with a screw

WATER-SCREW BOAT

balsa wood base

nail

rubber bands

rubber bands

paper clip

balsa wood base

bracket to hold propeller

bead

PADDLE BOAT
Connect the pieces together as shown to make a paddle.

CATAMARAN AND TRIMARAN

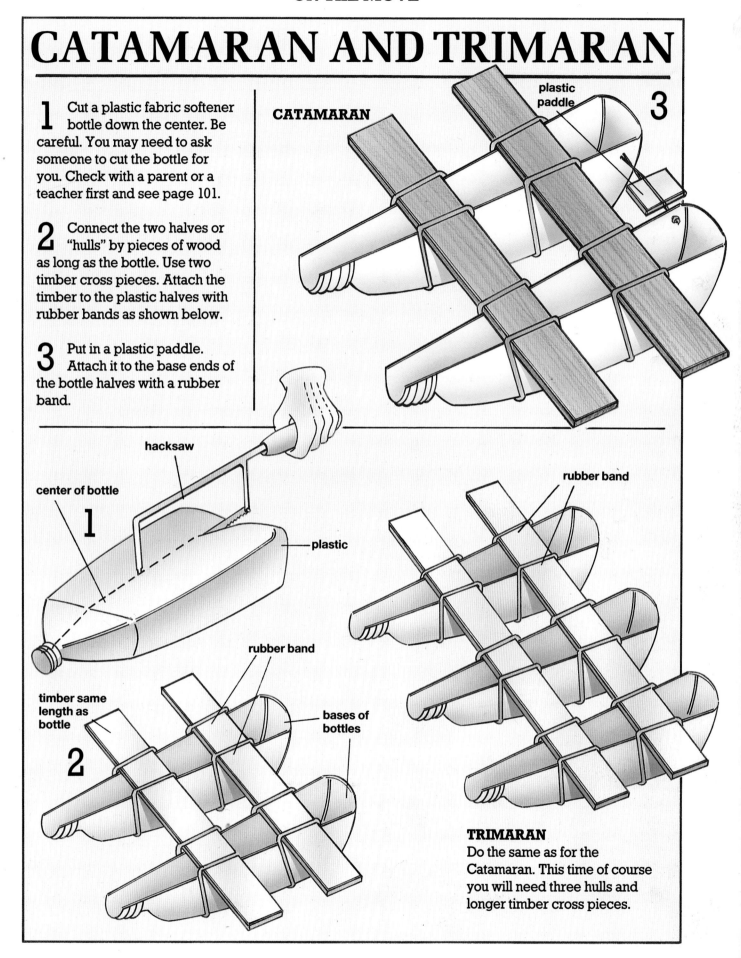

1 Cut a plastic fabric softener bottle down the center. Be careful. You may need to ask someone to cut the bottle for you. Check with a parent or a teacher first and see page 101.

2 Connect the two halves or "hulls" by pieces of wood as long as the bottle. Use two timber cross pieces. Attach the timber to the plastic halves with rubber bands as shown below.

3 Put in a plastic paddle. Attach it to the base ends of the bottle halves with a rubber band.

CATAMARAN

plastic paddle

3

hacksaw

center of bottle

1

plastic

timber same length as bottle

rubber band

2

bases of bottles

rubber band

TRIMARAN
Do the same as for the Catamaran. This time of course you will need three hulls and longer timber cross pieces.

67

101 SCIENCE TRICKS

NOTES FOR PARENTS AND TEACHERS

Pages 39 – 53   These are concerned with things in the air. If you want to consider the forces that keep paper planes in the air you will need to talk with children about thrust, drag, uplift and gravity. Thrust is provided by the airplane engine. In a paper plane, of course, it is provided by throwing. Drag is the resistance of the air to flight. It acts along the direction of motion of the airplane and opposes it. Lift is another force, it acts more or less perpendicularly to the direction of motion. The shape of an airplane wing helps develop lift. Gravity is the pull of the earth acting on the plane.

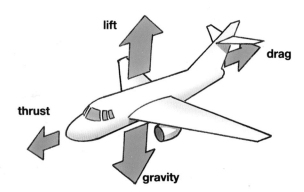

Page 45   Both the models on this page use a form of energy to make them move. The air escaping from the balloon causes it to move forward. To every action there is an equal and opposite reaction. When the balloon is blown up and closed, the air inside it presses equally in all directions. When the neck is released, the air rushes out and there is no longer any backward pressure. The forward pressure of air in the balloon remains the same however and it travels forward.

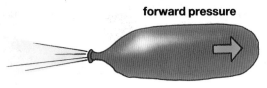

The propeller-driven plane moves on "rubber band energy." Children will have to put the "energy" in first by winding it up.

Pages 46 – 47   Air pressure is the operative force in making these two models work.

Page 48   The aerodynamics of boomerangs are extremely complex, which is not to say that children cannot get a "feel" for what is happening by playing with these models.

Page 49   Again we have a toy which works on air pressure.

Pages 50 – 51   The spinning blades from this helicopter cut the air and its curved shape gives it lift, much as an airplane wing does.

Do please supervise these activities.

Page 52   The kite, like the airplane, is subjected to the pull of gravity. The energy to lift it is provided by the wind, while the amount of that energy is determined by its angle to the wind.

Page 53   Hot-air balloons work on the principle that warm air is less dense than cold air (the molecules are further apart). Being filled with warm air, the balloons therefore tend to lift—displacing the colder, denser air above them.

Page 55   A toy that is very much concerned with "rubber band energy." If children are interested, you can experiment with the number of turns of the rubber band in relation to the distance travelled by each vehicle.

Page 56   Angle of attack of the wind is all important in getting a high speed from the land yacht – and it can travel! So encourage children to get the best angle with their boom.

Page 57   Introduces children to the idea of using an electric motor to make things move.

Pages 58 – 59   Both the jumping Jack and the mouse are based on the principle of the lever. That is to say, they are both dependent on the effect of a bar moving about a point.

Pages 60 – 63   You have to put energy into tops to make them spin. Colors in the surface of the top will blend. Theoretically, if you have a rainbow colored top all the colors should merge to give white. In practice, this is impossible since you cannot get pure enough pigments. At best you will get a grey blur. The same applies to the spinners.

Pages 64 – 65   There are lots of variables here for children to play with in order to get the best boat. Shapes of hull and sail, and power source whether it be blowing or propeller driven by elastic all come into effect.

Camphor reduces the surface tension of the water and the "water skin" in front of the boat pulls it forward.

3
on
Paper

INTRODUCTION

In **On Paper** you will find out about some of the amazing things that you can make and do with paper and cardboard.

Have you ever heard of paper making a noise? Try frightening your friends with a bull roarer!

Did you know that a simple fold in a piece of paper can help you to tell the time? Try making your very own pocket sundial.

Did you know that heat can make things move? Find out how to use heat to create a revolving ornament for the top of the Christmas tree.

Choosing a card to send to one of your friends is always a problem, so what about making some of your own, and making action ones at that!

Long ago the Ancient Chinese discovered lots of exciting ways of making interesting patterns with numbers and shapes. They even discovered some that they thought were magical. Try making them for yourself and see what you think.

These are just a few of the exciting things that you can make or do with paper.

PLAYING CARDS

Try building things with cards.

1 Build a house of cards. Lean two cards together to make a tent shape. Make another tent shape alongside and then put a card across the top. Continue in this way to build the bottom layer. Build a second layer on top of the first. Can you use all the cards in the pack without the house toppling over?

2 How tall a tower can you build with 6 cards as your base? How tall a tower can you build using just 3 cards as a base?

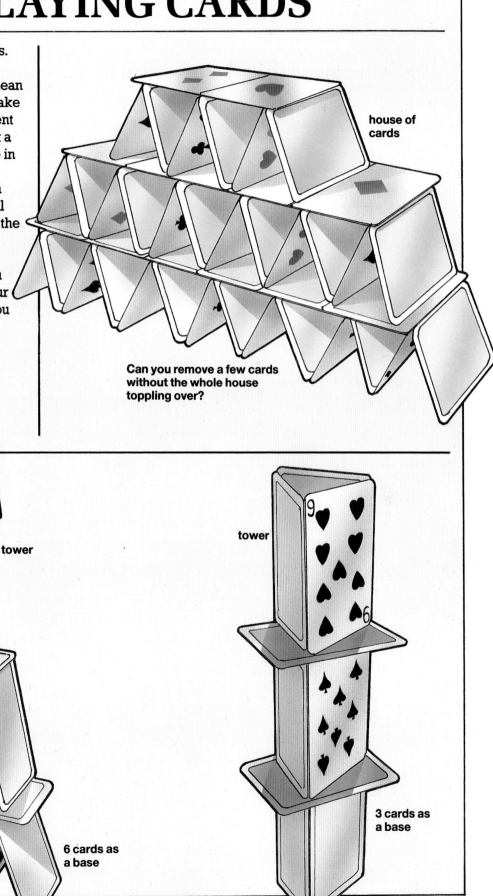

house of cards

Can you remove a few cards without the whole house toppling over?

tower

6 cards as a base

tower

3 cards as a base

BALANCING BILL

1 Trace the figure of Balancing Bill onto thick cardboard. Cut it out.

2 You will now need to balance him. Use a tightrope made from thin string tied between two plastic bottles filled with sand or soil. Attach Bill to the tightrope. He may balance; he may fall off. If he falls off, you need to make some counterbalances (see below).

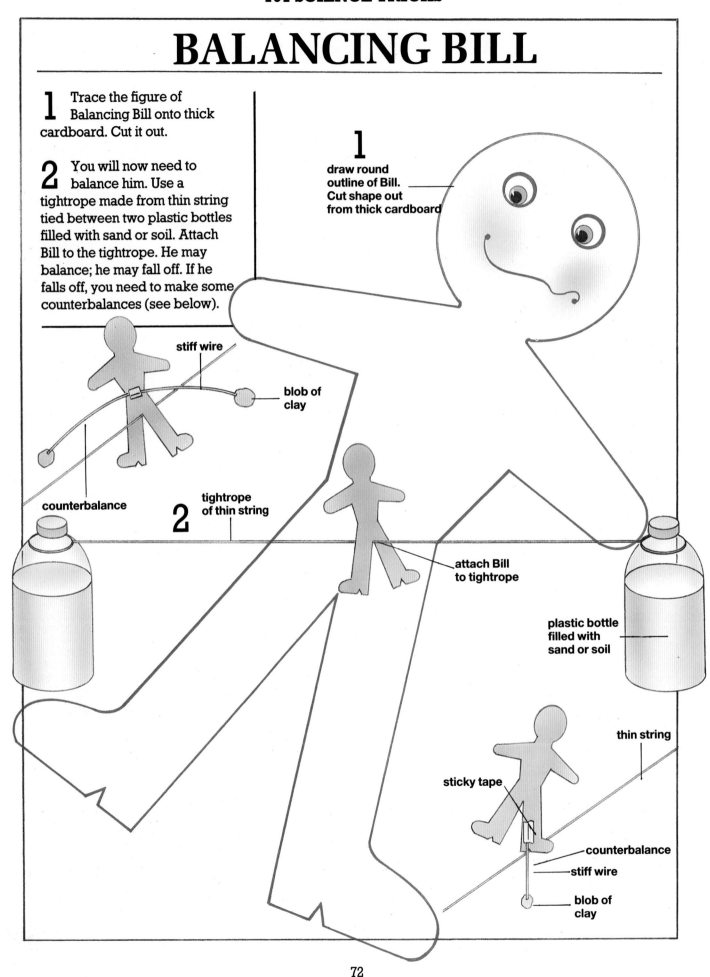

1 draw round outline of Bill. Cut shape out from thick cardboard

stiff wire

blob of clay

counterbalance

tightrope of thin string

2

attach Bill to tightrope

plastic bottle filled with sand or soil

thin string

sticky tape

counterbalance

stiff wire

blob of clay

BALANCING JILL

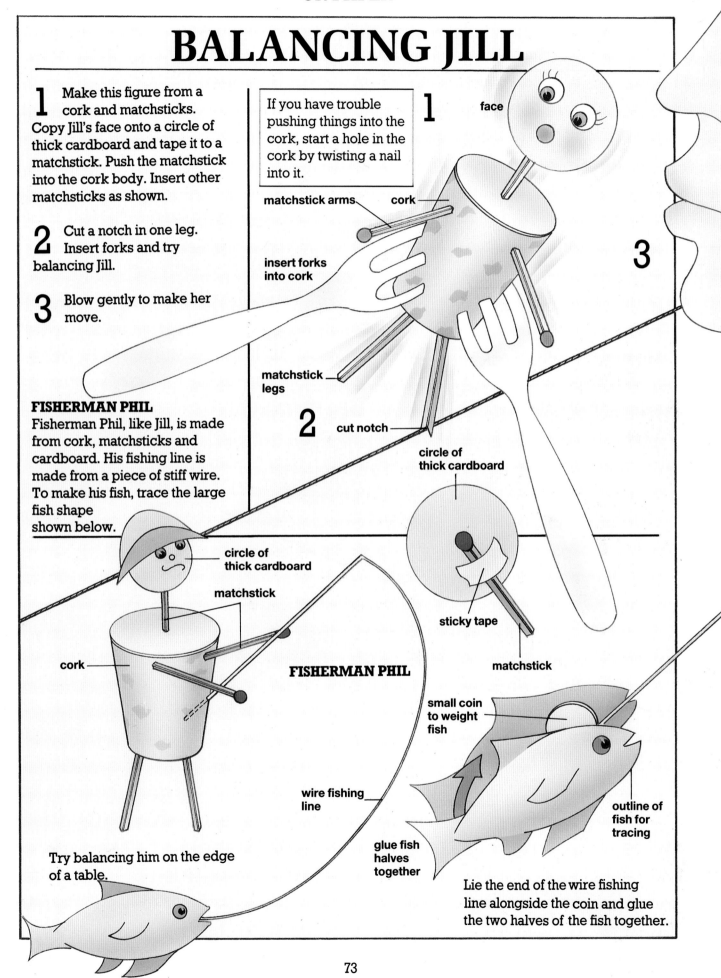

1 Make this figure from a cork and matchsticks. Copy Jill's face onto a circle of thick cardboard and tape it to a matchstick. Push the matchstick into the cork body. Insert other matchsticks as shown.

2 Cut a notch in one leg. Insert forks and try balancing Jill.

3 Blow gently to make her move.

If you have trouble pushing things into the cork, start a hole in the cork by twisting a nail into it.

1

face

matchstick arms

cork

insert forks into cork

matchstick legs

3

2 cut notch

circle of thick cardboard

circle of thick cardboard

sticky tape

matchstick

FISHERMAN PHIL

Fisherman Phil, like Jill, is made from cork, matchsticks and cardboard. His fishing line is made from a piece of stiff wire. To make his fish, trace the large fish shape shown below.

circle of thick cardboard

matchstick

cork

FISHERMAN PHIL

Try balancing him on the edge of a table.

wire fishing line

small coin to weight fish

glue fish halves together

outline of fish for tracing

Lie the end of the wire fishing line alongside the coin and glue the two halves of the fish together.

FEARSOME FRED

1 Trace and cut the large face of Fred from thick cardboard and color it in.

2 Balance him on the end of a ruler or the edge of a table as shown below. Use a paper clip to help you get him balanced. You need to move him about to find the best balancing point.

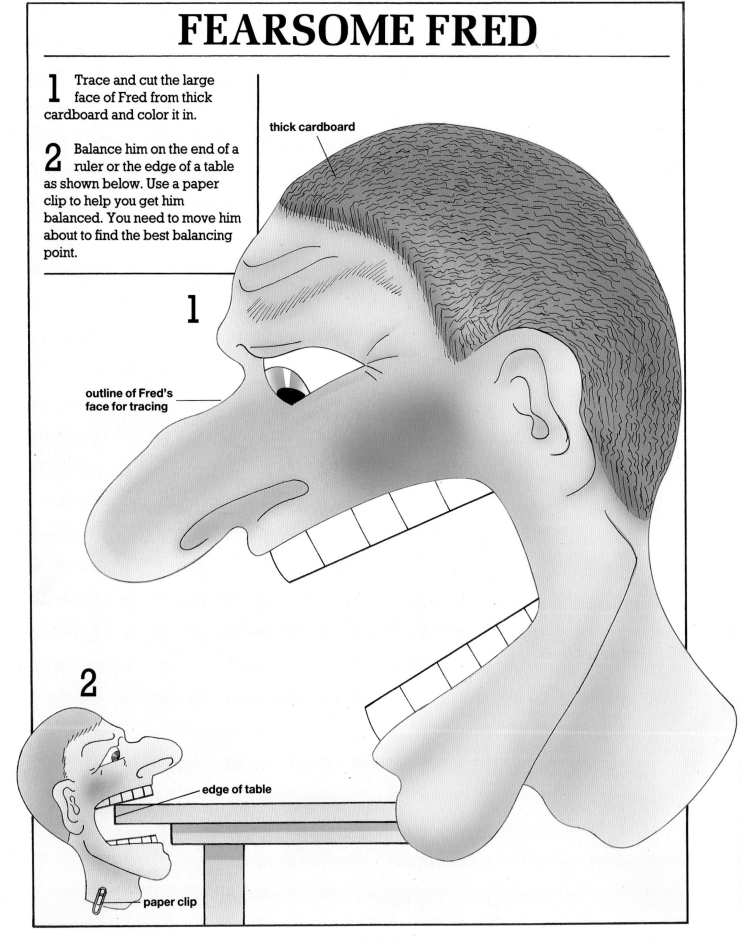

thick cardboard

1

outline of Fred's face for tracing

2

edge of table

paper clip

BALANCING BOYS

This toy is made from cardboard, balsa wood, wire and clay.

1 Shape a piece of balsa wood, as shown.

2 Draw and cut the see-saw and the two boys from cardboard. Color them in. Glue the boys to the see-saw and the see-saw to the balsa wood pivot.

3 Shape a bit of clay into a ball. Attach it to the stiff wire to make a counterweight as shown. This will help you get a good balance.

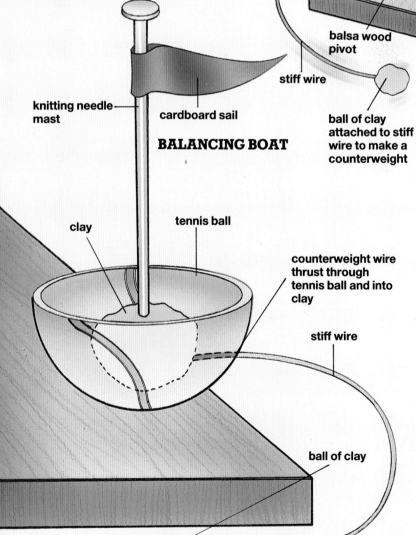

shape balsa wood to make pivot

card

bend here

glue boys to see-saw

balsa wood pivot

stiff wire

cardboard see-saw

knitting needle mast

cardboard sail

BALANCING BOAT

ball of clay attached to stiff wire to make a counterweight

clay

tennis ball

counterweight wire thrust through tennis ball and into clay

stiff wire

ball of clay

BALANCING BOAT

1 Cut an old tennis ball in half with tin snips (see page 101).

2 Make a counterweight from clay and wire as before.

3 Take another bit of clay and stick it inside the tennis ball. Thrust the wire of the counterweight through the tennis ball and into the clay.

4 Add a knitting needle mast and a cardboard sail, if you want.

You can probably make this balance without its counterweight if you are really sharp!

BULL ROARER

1 Cut a piece of heavy cardboard about 8 inches long by 2 inches wide. Round off the corners. Punch a hole at one end and thread a yard of string through. Knot it securely.

2 Twist the bull roarer so that you give it a slight bend.

3 Find a clear space. Swing it around your head. It will roar like a bull.

Decorate your bull roarer, if you want.

You could have a competition with your friends to see who can make the loudest bull roarer.

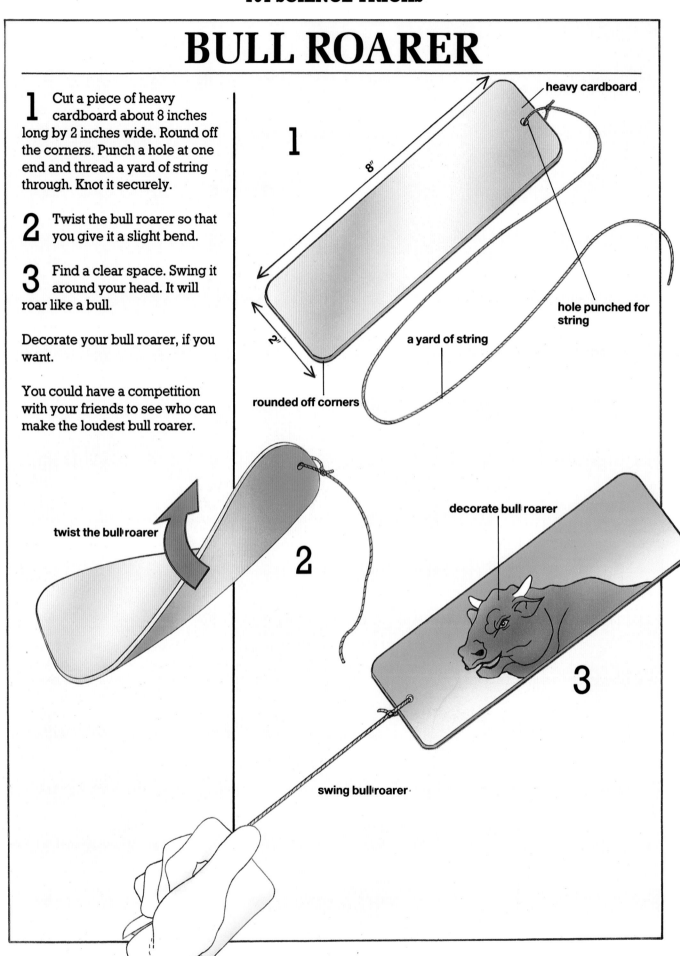

1

heavy cardboard

8"

hole punched for string

a yard of string

2"

rounded off corners

twist the bull roarer

2

decorate bull roarer

3

swing bull roarer

BUZZ SAW

1 Trace the buzz saw pattern below onto stiff cardboard. Color it in and cut it out.

2 Punch two holes through the cardboard. Use the point of a compass.

3 Thread a yard of thin string through the holes. Tie the ends.

4 Loop the ends of the string over your fingers. Pull the string outwards and then relax. Keep repeating this. The buzz saw will spin. Hold the revolving buzz saw to a sheet of paper sticking out from a table. As the teeth of the buzz saw hit the paper you will hear a buzzing noise.

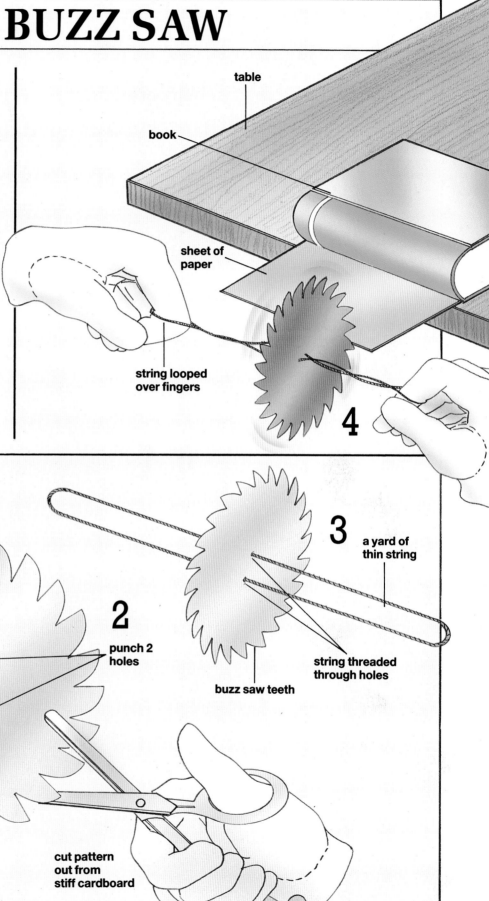

table

book

sheet of paper

string looped over fingers

4

3 a yard of thin string

2 punch 2 holes

string threaded through holes

buzz saw teeth

1 buzz saw pattern for tracing

cut pattern out from stiff cardboard

POCKET SUNDIAL

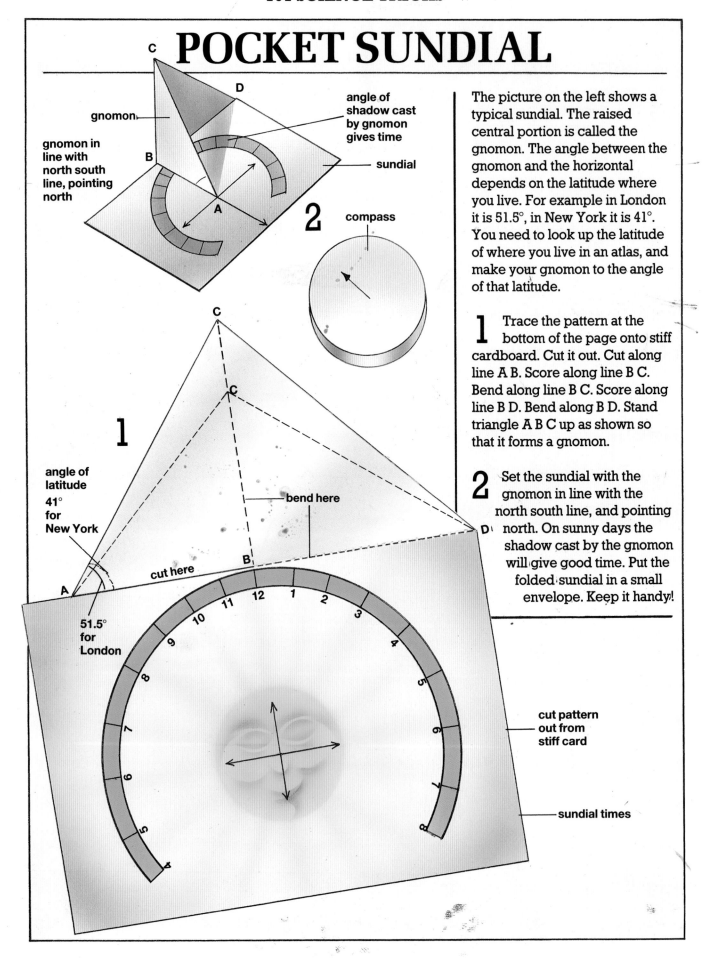

C

gnomon

D

angle of
shadow cast
by gnomon
gives time

gnomon in
line with
north south
line, pointing
north

B

sundial

A

2

compass

The picture on the left shows a
typical sundial. The raised
central portion is called the
gnomon. The angle between the
gnomon and the horizontal
depends on the latitude where
you live. For example in London
it is 51.5°, in New York it is 41°.
You need to look up the latitude
of where you live in an atlas, and
make your gnomon to the angle
of that latitude.

1 Trace the pattern at the
bottom of the page onto stiff
cardboard. Cut it out. Cut along
line A B. Score along line B C.
Bend along line B C. Score along
line B D. Bend along B D. Stand
triangle A B C up as shown so
that it forms a gnomon.

2 Set the sundial with the
gnomon in line with the
north south line, and pointing
north. On sunny days the
shadow cast by the gnomon
will give good time. Put the
folded sundial in a small
envelope. Keep it handy!

C

1

C

angle of
latitude
41°
for
New York

bend here

B

cut here

D

A

51.5°
for
London

cut pattern
out from
stiff card

11 12 1 2 3 4 5 6 7
10
9
8
7
6
5
4

sundial times

STAR CLOCK

1 Cut a 6″ disc from cardboard and draw a 4″ circle on it. Mark out 30 degree sectors with a protractor on the 4″ circle. Draw in the Big Dipper, Cassiopeia and the North Star as shown.
snown.

2 Cut an 8″ disc from cardboard and draw a 6″ circle on it. Mark out a 24 hour clock on this large disc.

3 Fix the small disc to the large disc with a paper fastener. At night match the star circle with the Big Dipper constellation in the sky. Note the time and arrange the clock circle against the pointers of the Dipper.

An hour later check the position of the Big Dipper. Match the star circle to the Big Dipper again. You will find it rotates around your 24 hour clock.

2

8″ diameter

6″

mark out a 24-hour clock on the large disc

3

Big Dipper

The North Star

paper fastener

Cassiopeia

1

4″

mark out 30° sectors

paper fastener

6″ diameter

79

REVOLVING SNAKE

1 Trace this snake onto thick stiff paper.

2 Cut it out. Cut along the line of the snake.

3 Make a pinprick through the snake's tail.

Put thread through the hole. Tie two or three knots.

4 Hold the snake above the table lamp. The heat current rising from the lamp will cause the snake to revolve.

A snake hung above a radiator will turn all day – if the radiator is left on.

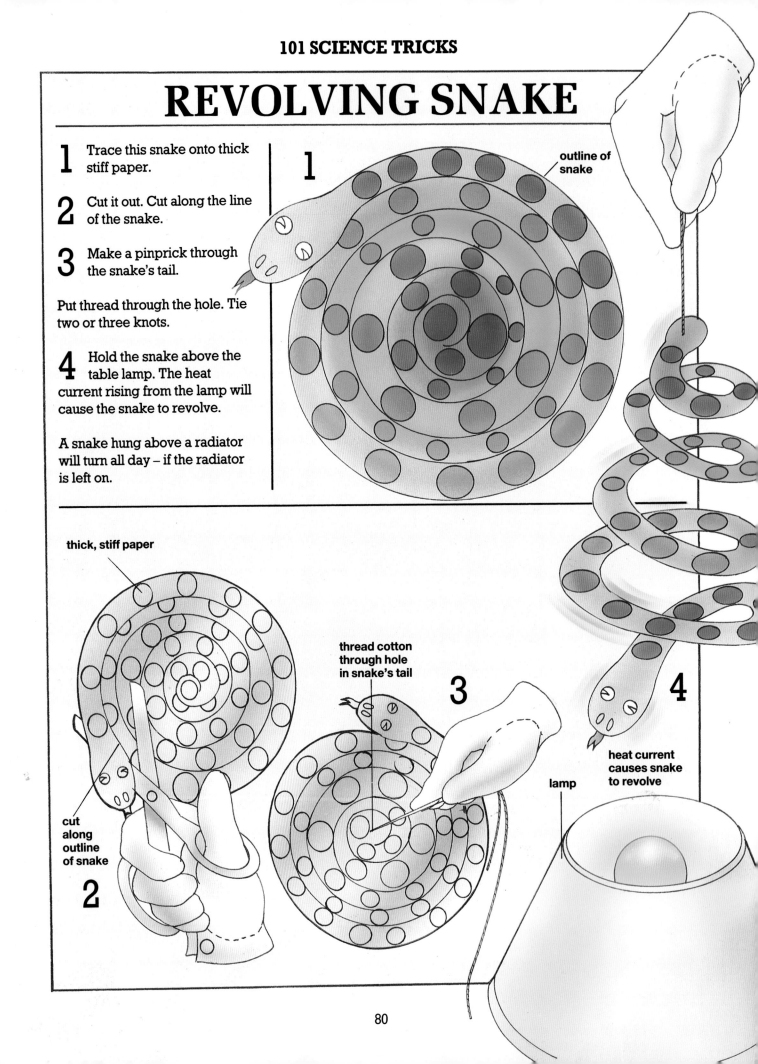

1

outline of snake

thick, stiff paper

cut along outline of snake

2

thread cotton through hole in snake's tail

3

4

heat current causes snake to revolve

lamp

CHRISTMAS TREE ANGEL

Cut a snake as before but this time use aluminum kitchen foil.

1 Trace the shape shown below. Cut this from kitchen foil too but make it double thickness for strength.

2 Leave an extended piece that can be bent back to make a base.

3 Use a grommet as a bearing. Stick it to the base of the angel with a touch of glue.

4 Stick the foil snake to the grommet by its head. Use a needle pushed into the end of a balsa wood rod as a pivot.

The figure will revolve well on the Christmas Tree if a few small lights are put just beneath it.

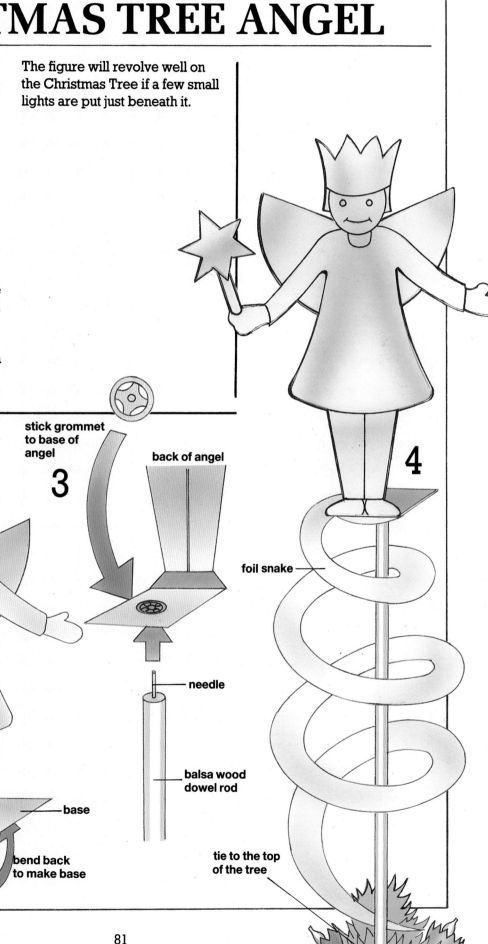

outline of angel

1

2 layers of aluminum foil

stick grommet to base of angel

3

back of angel

4

foil snake

needle

balsa wood dowel rod

base

bend back to make base

2

extended piece

tie to the top of the tree

MAGIC SQUARES

Magic squares were invented many centuries ago by the Chinese. The earliest form is shown on the right, the "lo-shu," as it is called. Can you see what is magic about it? Count the dots in each row, column and both diagonals.

1 Whether you add up, down or across, the answer always comes to 15 — three times the center number.

This square is so magical that some people still wear it as a lucky charm. This is an "order 3" magic square since it has 3 rows and 3 columns. You can make lots of order 3 squares to try on your friends.

2 Add 3 to every number in the original square.

The answers to the additions are now 24 — three times the center number.

Try adding other numbers.

3 Multiply every number in the original square by 4.

The answer to the additions is 60 — three times the center number.

Try multiplying by other numbers.

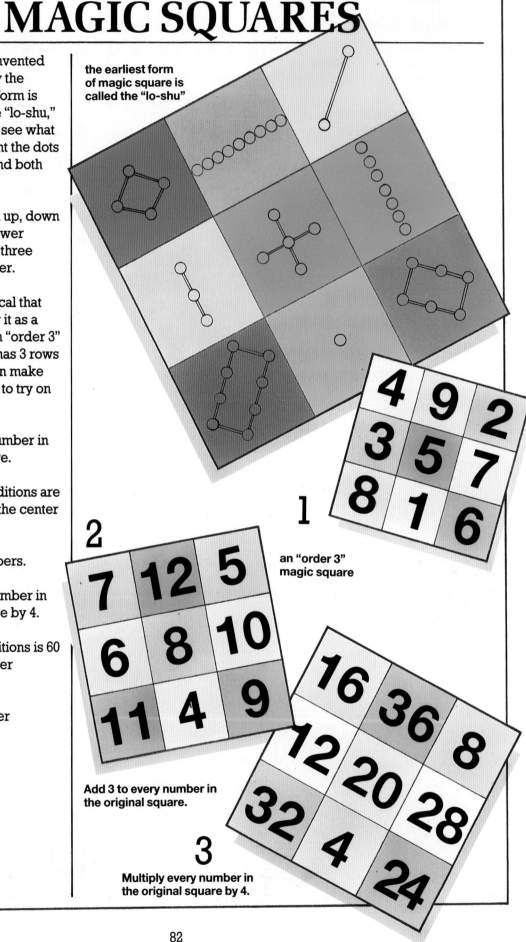

the earliest form of magic square is called the "lo-shu"

4	9	2
3	5	7
8	1	6

1 an "order 3" magic square

2

7	12	5
6	8	10
11	4	9

Add 3 to every number in the original square.

16	36	8
12	20	28
32	4	24

3 Multiply every number in the original square by 4.

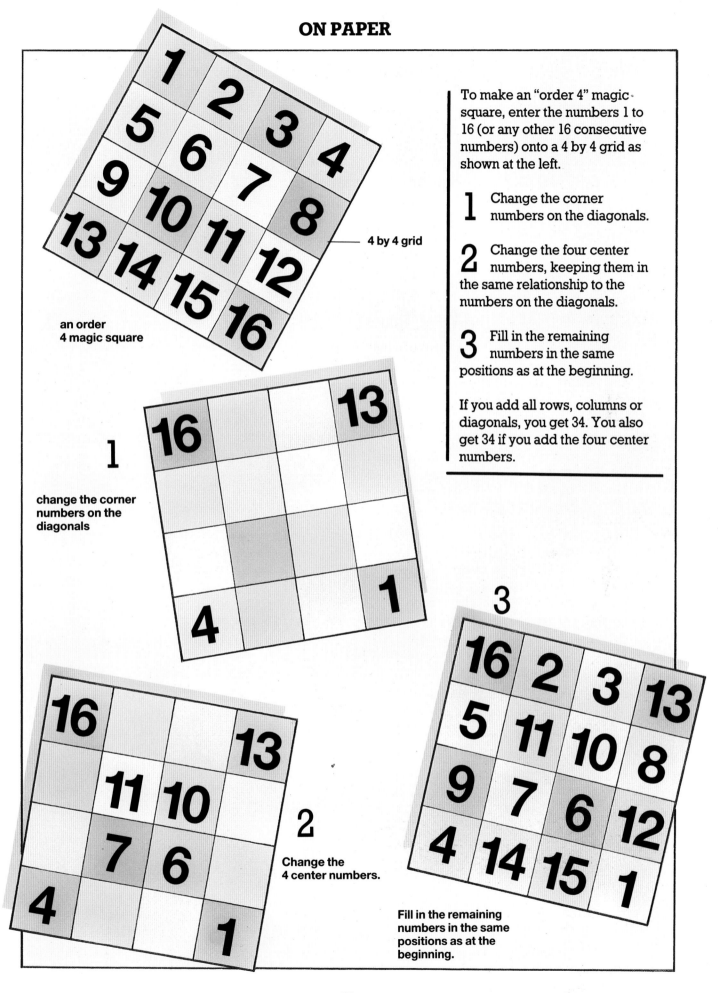

an order
4 magic square

4 by 4 grid

To make an "order 4" magic square, enter the numbers 1 to 16 (or any other 16 consecutive numbers) onto a 4 by 4 grid as shown at the left.

1 Change the corner numbers on the diagonals.

2 Change the four center numbers, keeping them in the same relationship to the numbers on the diagonals.

3 Fill in the remaining numbers in the same positions as at the beginning.

If you add all rows, columns or diagonals, you get 34. You also get 34 if you add the four center numbers.

1

change the corner numbers on the diagonals

2

Change the 4 center numbers.

3

Fill in the remaining numbers in the same positions as at the beginning.

TANGRAMS

Another Chinese invention is the tangram. It is a seven piece puzzle.

1 It is easy to construct if you use the sixteen square grid shown to help you draw the seven pieces. These then need to be cut out. You could color them in, if you like.

2 Can you remake the square from the seven pieces?

3 The Chinese use the pieces to make all sorts of figures like the examples below. You try.

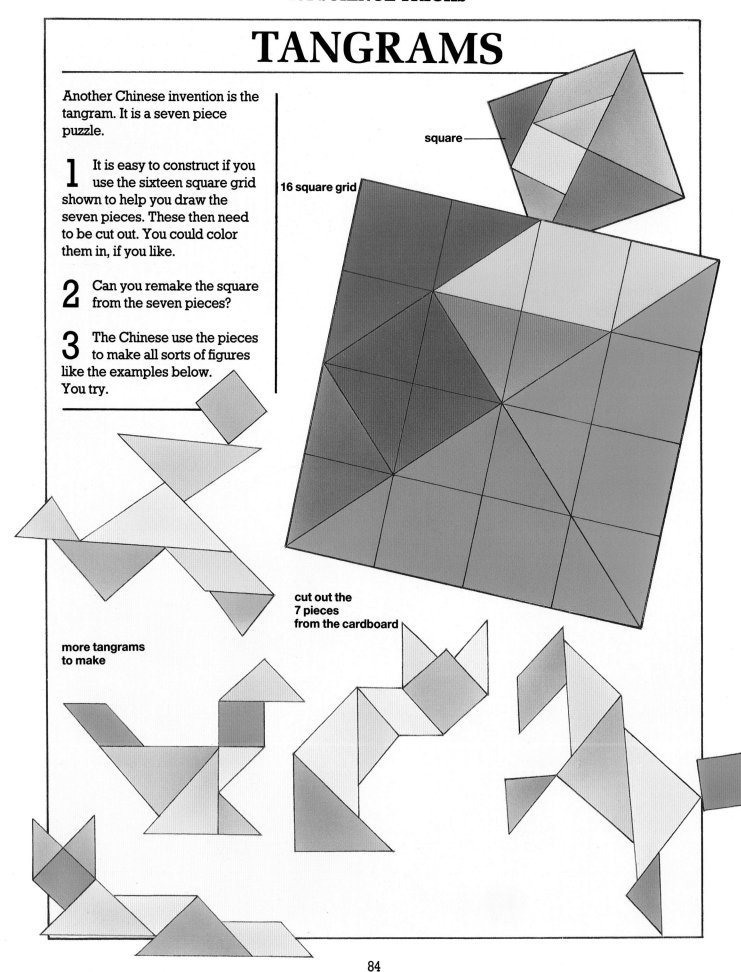

square

16 square grid

cut out the
7 pieces
from the cardboard

more tangrams
to make

MAGIC EGGS

1 Trace the pattern of the magic egg onto cardboard.

2 Cut out the seven pieces and color them in.

3 What birds can you hatch using your seven pieces?

magic egg for tracing

color in pieces

7 pieces

Can you make any other birds with your 7 pieces?

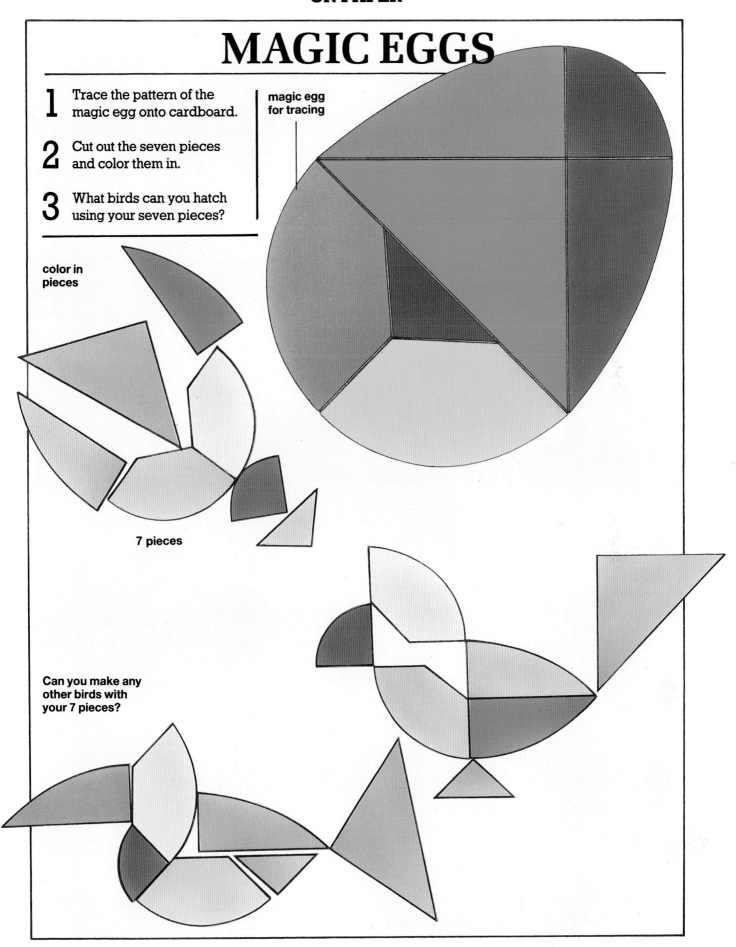

3-D DESK CALENDAR

1 Trace this 5-sided shape called a pentagon onto cardboard. Cut it out to make a template.

2 On thick paper or thin card draw around the template to construct the two models shown below. Remember to draw the flaps too.

3 Cut out the models. Fold all the flaps and score along all the sides of the inner pentagon.

4 Glue the two models together to make a 12-sided shape called a dodecahedron.

5 Each face of the dodecahedron will hold the calendar for one month of the year. Write one month on each face. You may find it easier to write up your calendar before you join the two models together.

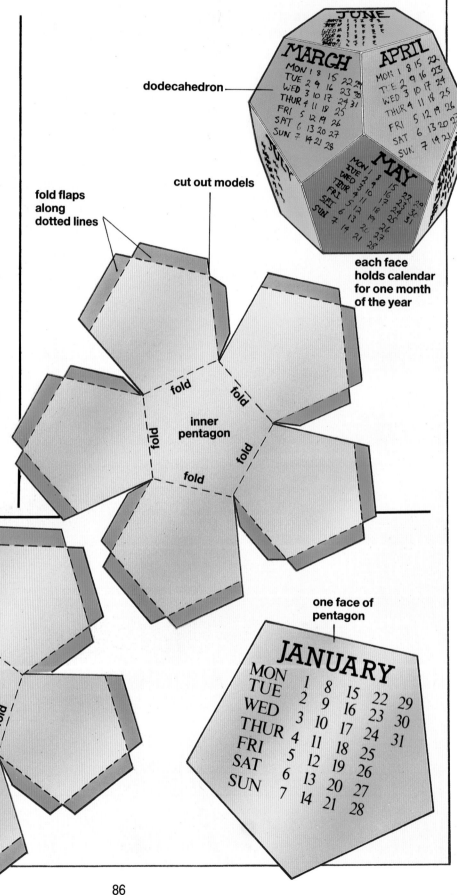

dodecahedron

each face holds calendar for one month of the year

fold flaps along dotted lines

cut out models

fold

fold

fold

fold

fold

inner pentagon

fold

fold

fold

fold

fold

fold

one face of pentagon

JANUARY

MON	1	8	15	22	29
TUE	2	9	16	23	30
WED	3	10	17	24	31
THUR	4	11	18	25	
FRI	5	12	19	26	
SAT	6	13	20	27	
SUN	7	14	21	28	

OTHER 3-D SHAPES

The dodecahedron is a regular solid. There are four other regular solids: the cube, tetrahedron, octahedron and icosahedron. The models for each of these solids are shown below.

1 Trace each model onto thin cardboard. Cut it out. Score along all the dotted lines.

2 Shape and glue each solid. When they are made you can hang them by thread from a shelf. You can hang a dodecahedron too.

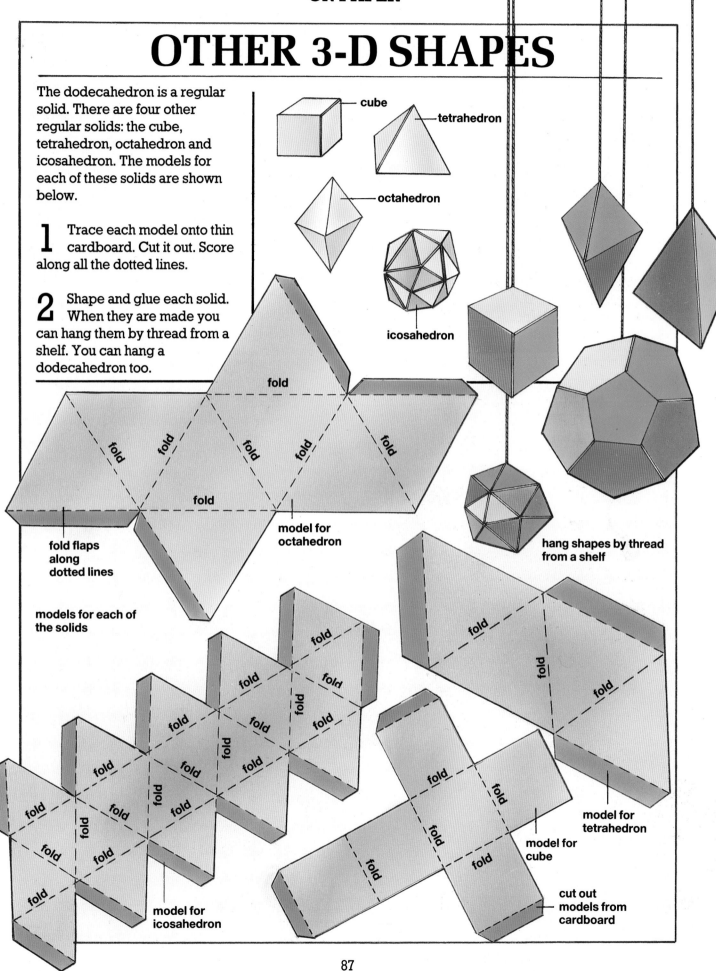

cube

tetrahedron

octahedron

icosahedron

fold

fold

fold

fold

fold

fold

fold

fold flaps
along
dotted lines

models for each of
the solids

model for
octahedron

hang shapes by thread
from a shelf

fold

fold

fold

fold

fold

fold

fold

fold

fold

fold

fold

fold

fold

fold

fold

fold

fold

fold

fold

fold

fold

fold

fold

fold

fold

model for
tetrahedron

model for
cube

model for
icosahedron

cut out
models from
cardboard

87

CHRISTMAS CARD

1 Trace and cut out these four templates A, B, C, D from card.

2 Cut out the two slits in template D as shown.

3 Color in Santa Claus, template A.

4 Thread the long narrow strip (C) through the two slits in the large card D. Stick Santa Claus to the top of strip C. Lightly glue the fireplace B to each side of the card. Let it dry.

5 Pull on the strip to make Santa Claus appear. Push on the strip to send him back up the chimney. Decorate the front of the chimney.

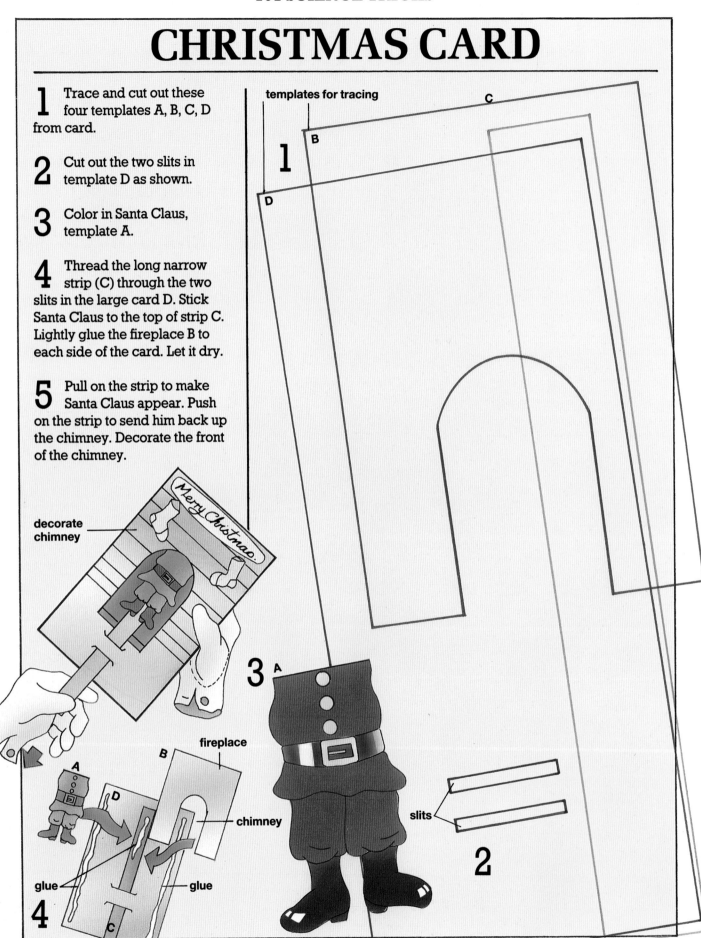

templates for tracing

decorate chimney

Merry Christmas

fireplace

chimney

slits

glue

glue

GET WELL CARD

1 Trace and cut these templates A B C below from cardboard. Cut out the shaded portions on the large card A.

2 Draw the mouse on the narrow strip of card C.

3 Fasten the small card oblong B to the back of the large card A with a touch of glue at top and bottom.

Assemble.

4 Push and pull the strip to make the mouse appear and disappear.

Decorate the card.

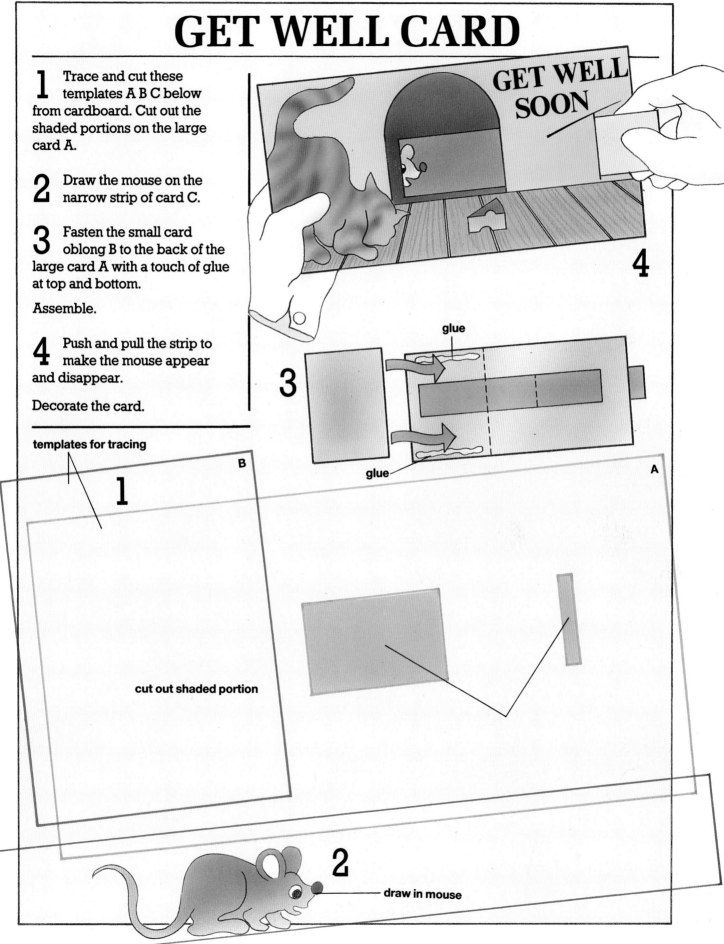

GET WELL SOON

4

3

glue

glue

templates for tracing

1

B

A

cut out shaded portion

2

draw in mouse

NEW YEAR CARD

1 Trace the three templates A B C onto cardboard. Cut them out. Cut slits in template A, one long slit and one curved slit, as shown below.

2 Fasten the T-shaped template B to the main card A with a paper fastener. The long arm of the T should protrude through the long slit, and the short arm should stick through the curved slit.

3 Stick the bell to the short protruding arm. Moving the long arm will make the bell move.

4 Decorate the card and ring in the New Year.

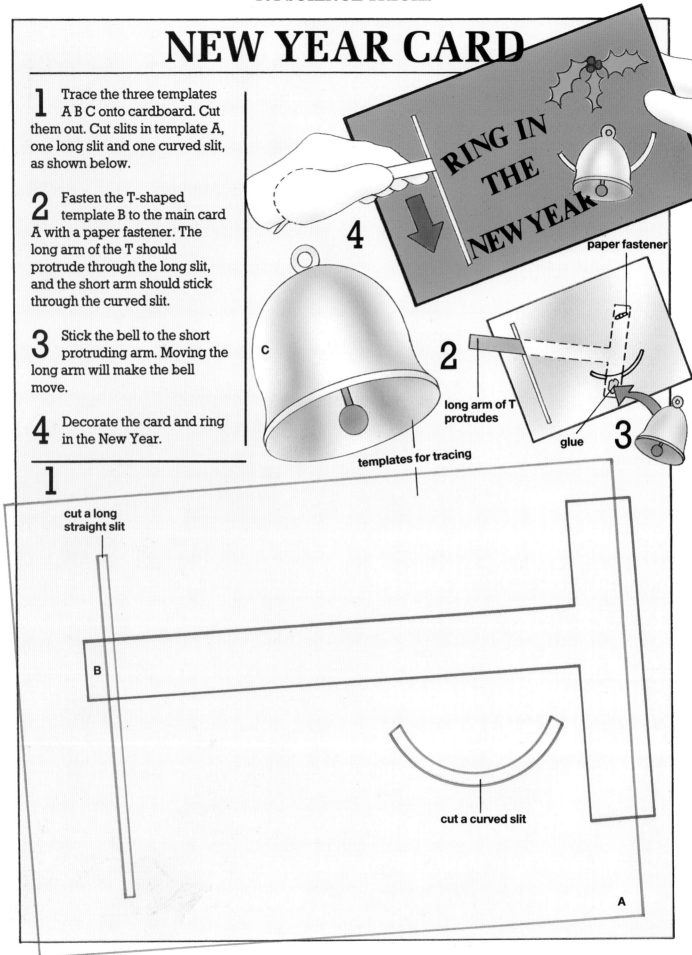

RING IN THE NEW YEAR

paper fastener

long arm of T protrudes

glue

2

3

4

C

templates for tracing

1

cut a long straight slit

B

cut a curved slit

A

MOBILES

Balancing structures like these are called mobiles. Try making one from string and plant stalks or twigs. You can tie on all sorts of things. Always begin balancing from the bottom up.

1 Take one stalk. Tie a piece of string at its center. Balance the stalk from this string and then add objects on either side of the string, carefully adjusting them so that you get a balance.

2 Do the same thing with a separate stalk. Now tie these two stalks to a stalk dangling above them.

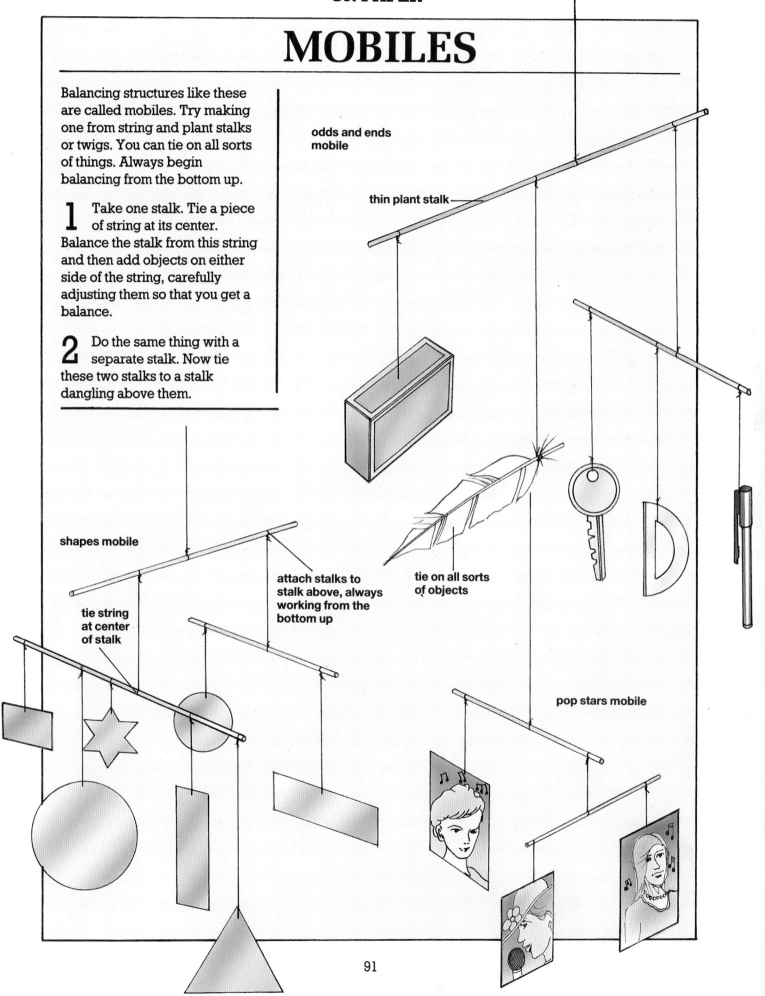

odds and ends
mobile

thin plant stalk

shapes mobile

tie string
at center
of stalk

attach stalks to
stalk above, always
working from the
bottom up

tie on all sorts
of objects

pop stars mobile

91

TWO-WAY PICTURE

1 Choose two full-color magazine pictures. Make sure they are both exactly the same size, or cut them to the same size.

2 Take a piece of thin cardboard the same height as the magazine clippings. Fold it into accordion pleats half an inch wide. Cut picture one into half-inch strips.

3 Glue these half inch strips each in turn onto the left-facing pleats. Cut the second picture into half-inch strips and again glue these in turn onto the right-facing pleats.

If you look at your accordion folder from the left you will see one picture. If you view it from the right you will see the other.

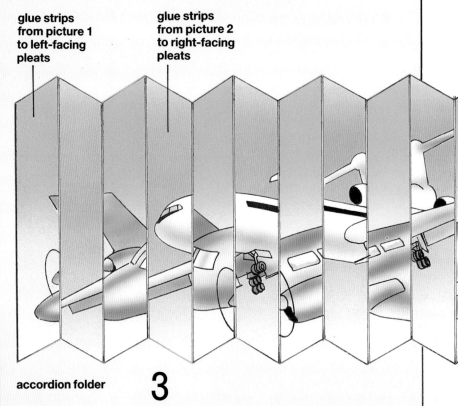

glue strips from picture 1 to left-facing pleats

glue strips from picture 2 to right-facing pleats

accordion folder **3**

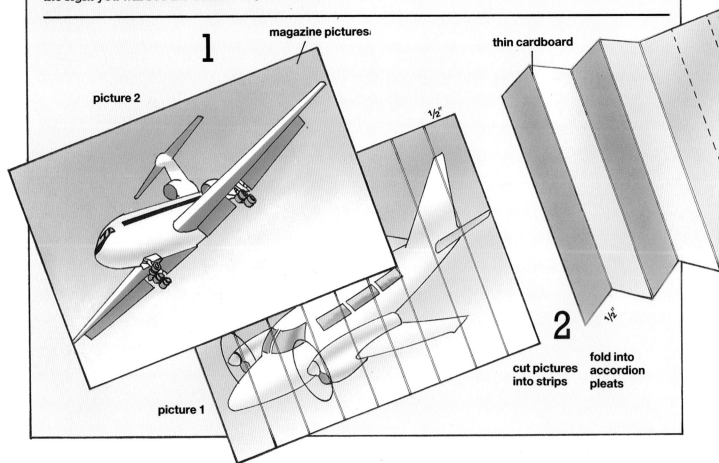

1

magazine pictures

picture 2

picture 1

thin cardboard

½"

½"

2

cut pictures into strips

fold into accordion pleats

THREE-WAY PICTURE

1 For this, you need three magazine pictures. Again they must all be the same size. Number your pictures 1–3.

2 Cut a piece of cardboard to the same height and the total length of the three pictures. Crease the card into half-inch lengths. Number them 1, 2, 3; 1, 2, 3. . . as shown.

3 Bend the card so that it looks like "pattern X," shown below.

4 Cut each magazine picture into half-inch strips. Glue strips from your picture 1 to the card wherever the number 1 is shown. You will see that this means gluing the first strip at the edge, missing two strips of card, then gluing in the next picture strip. Continue gluing one and missing two until you finish picture.

Glue strips from pictures 2 and 3 in the same way in the positions shown.

5 Fold the accordion so that every third strip remains flat.

View the accordion folder from the left to see one picture, from the front to see another, and from the right to see yet another.

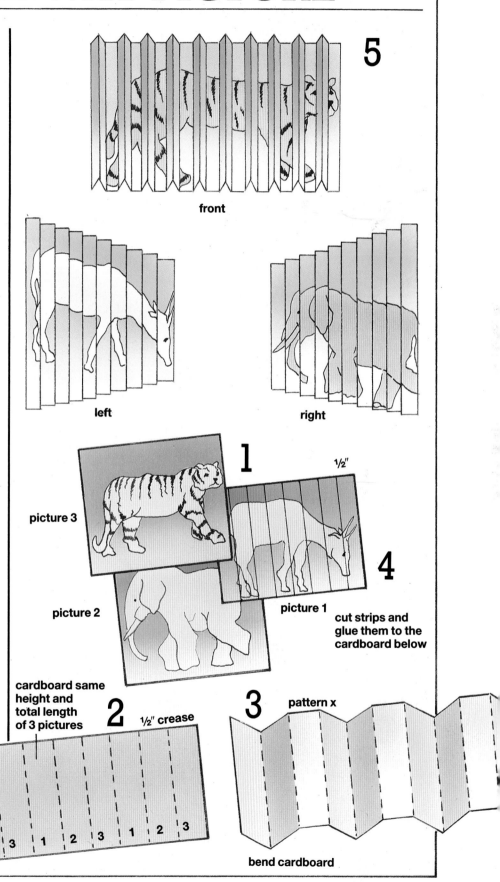

5

front

left

right

1

½″

picture 3

picture 2

picture 1

4

cut strips and glue them to the cardboard below

cardboard same height and total length of 3 pictures

2 ½″ crease

1 2 3 1 2 3 1 2 3 1 2 3 1 2 3

3 pattern x

bend cardboard

POP UP CARDS

Greeting cards that pop up when you open them are very popular.

They are easy to make.

1 Trace the balloon and butterfly onto thin cardboard. Color them in and cut them out.

2 Trace two copies of the V shape and cut these from cardboard too. Score each V shape along the dotted lines.

3 Take sheets of thin cardboard and fold them to make your greeting cards. Fold and glue your V shape into the folded card as shown.

4 Glue the long "tail" of the butterfly as illustrated.

5 Attach the balloon with a bit of thread and glue.

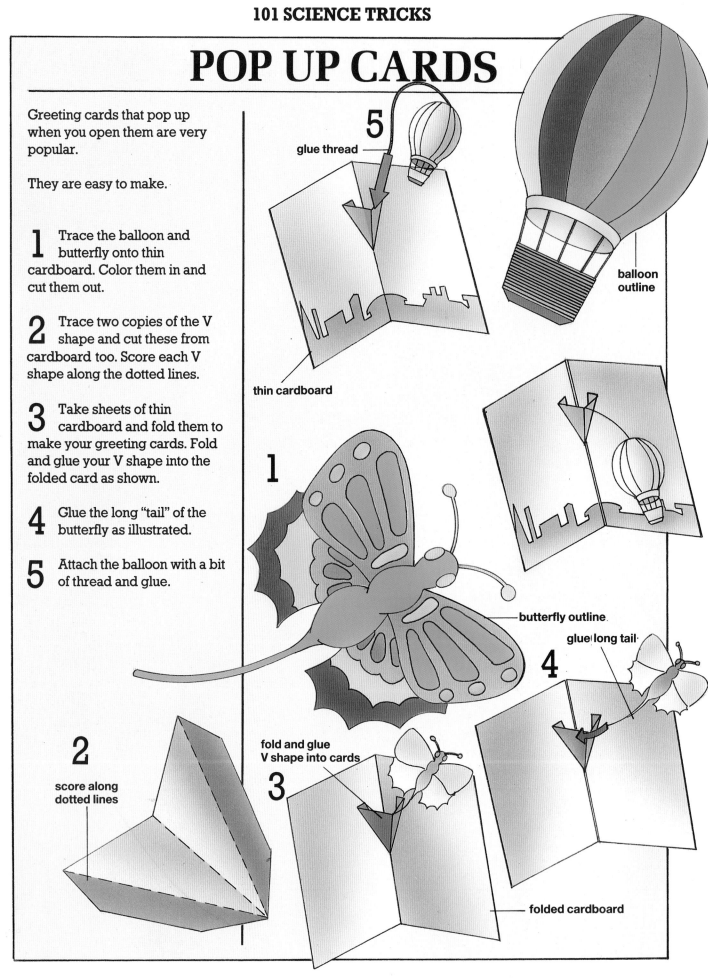

5 glue thread

thin cardboard

balloon outline

1 butterfly outline

glue long tail

4

fold and glue V shape into cards

3

2 score along dotted lines

folded cardboard

PICTURE PATTERNS

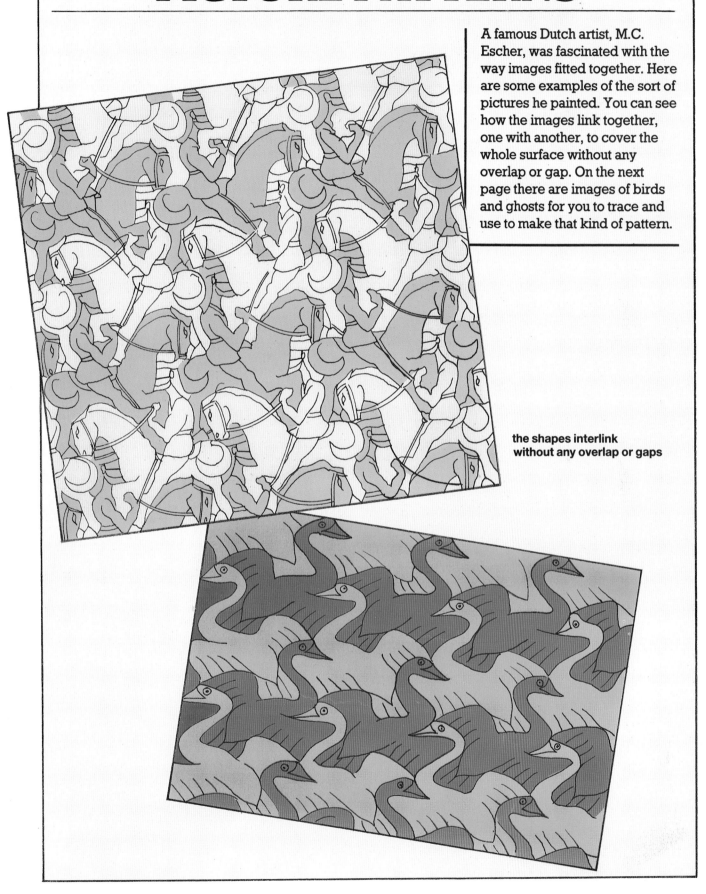

A famous Dutch artist, M.C. Escher, was fascinated with the way images fitted together. Here are some examples of the sort of pictures he painted. You can see how the images link together, one with another, to cover the whole surface without any overlap or gap. On the next page there are images of birds and ghosts for you to trace and use to make that kind of pattern.

the shapes interlink
without any overlap or gaps

BIRDS

1 Trace a number of these birds onto thin cardboard.

2 Color them in bright colors and cut them out and fit them into an interlinking pattern, as M.C. Escher did in his paintings.

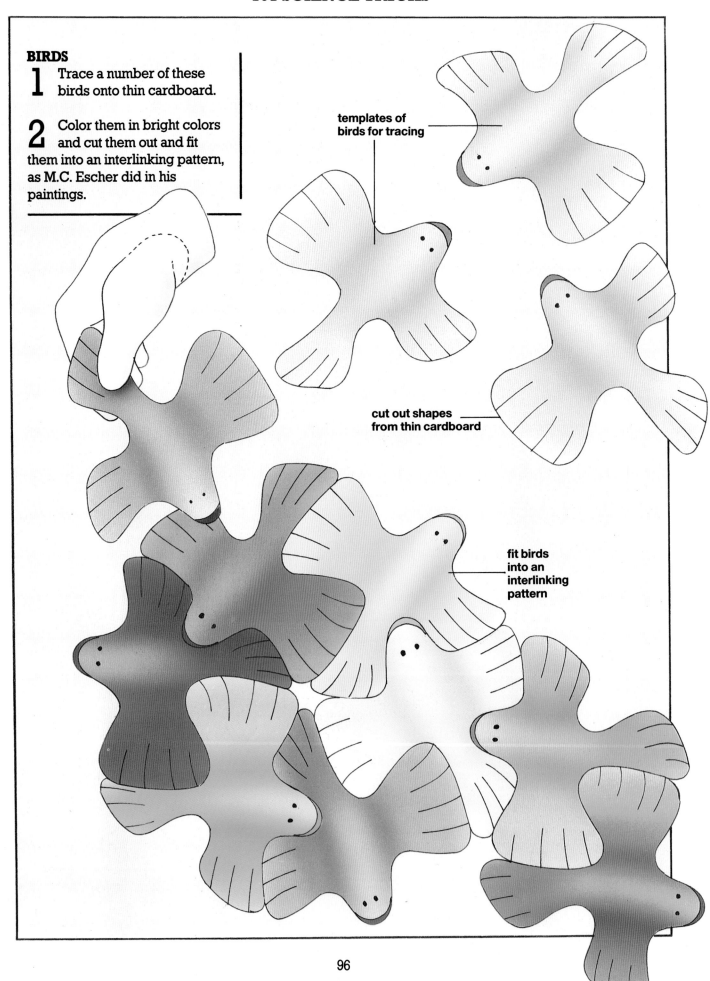

templates of birds for tracing

cut out shapes from thin cardboard

fit birds into an interlinking pattern

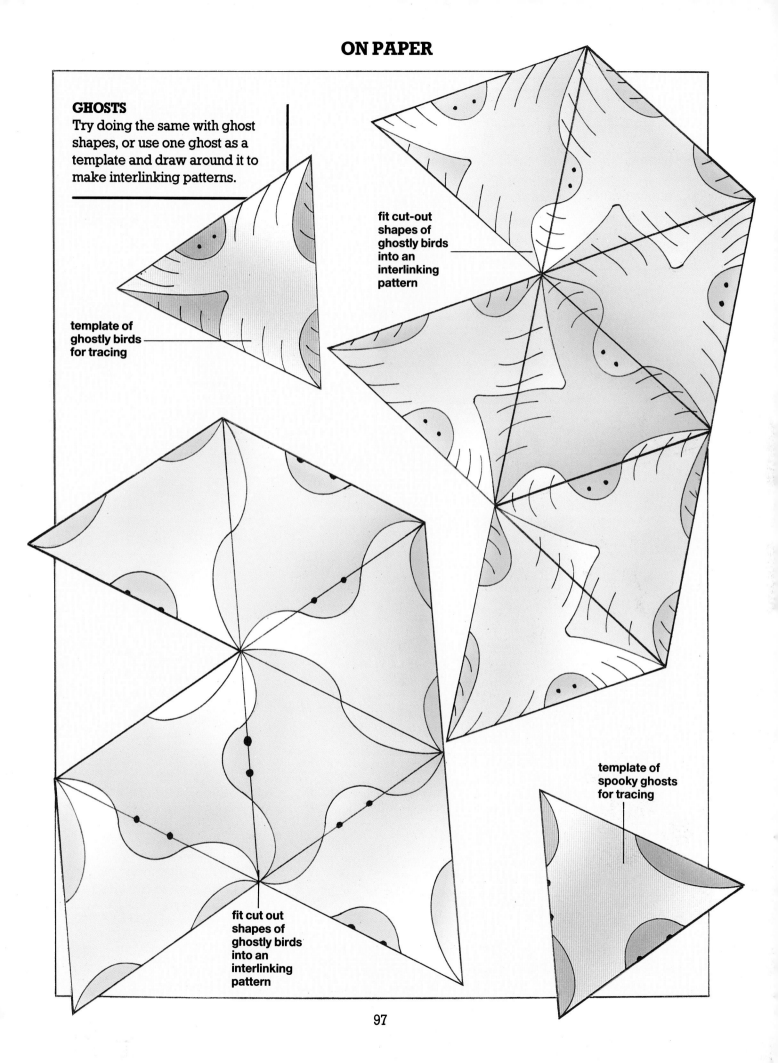

GHOSTS

Try doing the same with ghost shapes, or use one ghost as a template and draw around it to make interlinking patterns.

fit cut-out shapes of ghostly birds into an interlinking pattern

template of ghostly birds for tracing

fit cut out shapes of ghostly birds into an interlinking pattern

template of spooky ghosts for tracing

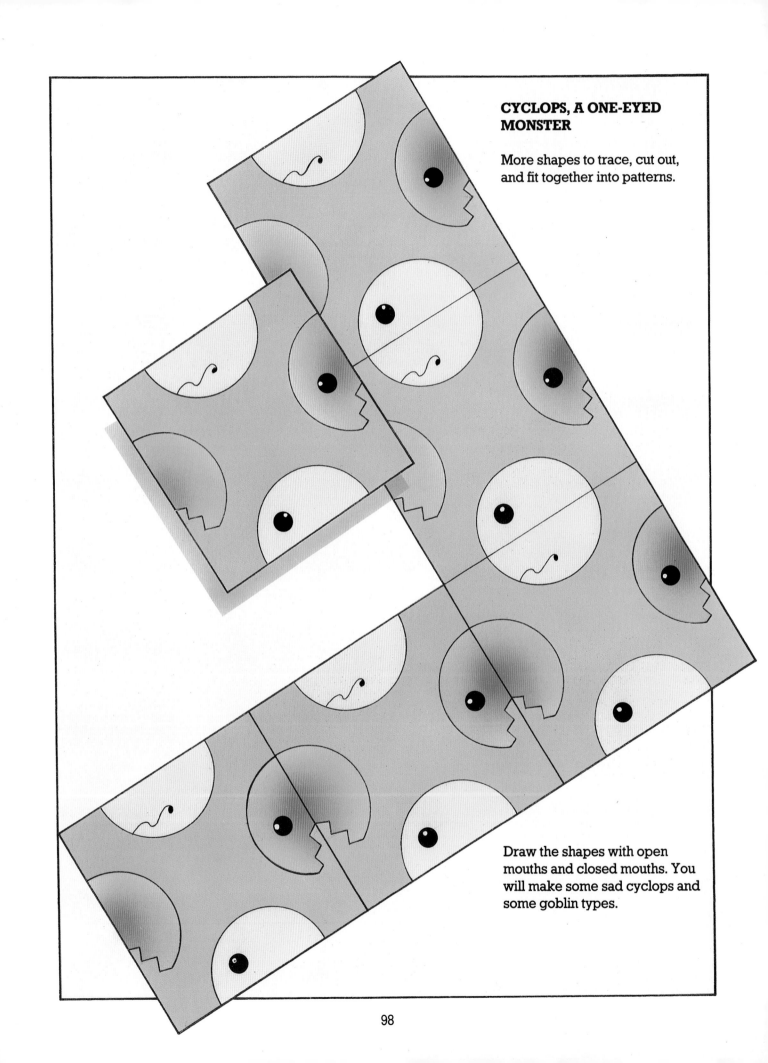

CYCLOPS, A ONE-EYED MONSTER

More shapes to trace, cut out, and fit together into patterns.

Draw the shapes with open mouths and closed mouths. You will make some sad cyclops and some goblin types.

PLUMBER'S NIGHTMARE

You can make more complex
designs, as this pattern shows.

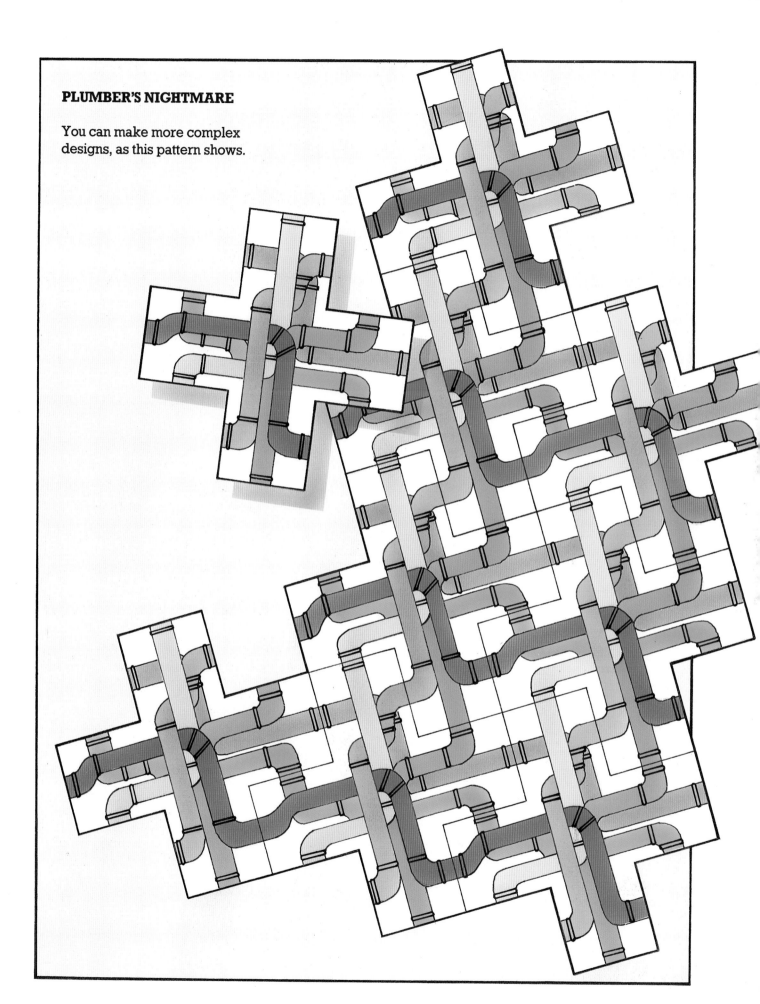

101 SCIENCE TRICKS

NOTES FOR PARENTS AND TEACHERS

Pages 71 – 75 Things fall because of a force of attraction towards the center of the earth. We are constantly adjusting our center of gravity, mostly unconsciously, as we move. Originally, as very small children, we had to learn how to do this. These pages are concerned with center of gravity games and toys, being concerned with how to get a balance about a central point.

Pages 76 – 77 Children are learning that sounds are produced by vibrating objects. You do not get a sound without making something vibrate.

Page 76 The bull roarer vibrates when spun, making its peculiar noise.

Page 77 The buzz saw causes the paper to vibrate, making a high-pitched sound.

Pages 78 – 79 These pages describe two clocks. In one we tell the time by the sun, in the other by the stars. Children's attention will be drawn to the apparent daily motion of both sun and stars. They will realize that the day length changes throughout the year and be able to measure time using their clocks.

Page 78 The sundial shown is a typical sundial. The raised central portion is called the gnomon. The angle of the gnomon to the horizontal varies with the latitude of where you live. For example in London it is $51.5°$, while in New York it is $41°$.

The graduations on the sundial are not an equal distance apart.

This table gives their position.

Sundial Time	Angle Between Numerals
6 am	0
7	19
8	36.5
9	52
10	65.5
11	78
12	90
1 pm	102
2	114.5
3	128
4	143.5
5	161
6	180

The 4 am and 5 am marks are diametrically opposite the 4 pm and 5 pm marks; with the 7 pm and 8 pm marks diametrically opposite the 7 am and 8 am ones.

This table may not be correct for where you live. Look up your latitude in an atlas. Make your gnomon to the angle of that latitude. Choose a sunny day! Set up your sundial and plot the angles of the shadows cast on the hour through the day. You can then measure the angles formed and make a table like the one shown above.

Page 79 This clock will, of course, rotate counter-clockwise, since the stars appear to spin in a counter-clockwise manner. In the southern hemisphere you need to choose different constellations.

Pages 80 – 81 Both these models illustrate how warm air rises; that is, they work on convection currents.

Pages 82 – 83 Magic squares show how intriguing numbers can be. At the same time they illustrate that numbers do not work in a helter-skelter way but in patterns. Looking for patterns is at the heart of mathematics.

Pages 84 – 85 Tangrams give children scope for inventing all sorts of patterns and figures, and at the same time help develop the concept of area as amount of surface covered.

Pages 86 – 87 The 3D structures described on these pages are the Platonic solids. They are the only regular solids. They were invented by Plato, and the Greeks used them as symbols: tetrahedron (fire), octahedron (air), cube (earth), icosahedron (water), dodecahedron (universe).

Pages 88 – 91 The cards and the mobiles all use levers as their working principle. That is to say, they all use a bar turning about a point.

Pages 92 – 93 Two and three way pictures like these greatly intrigued our great-grandparents. Making them draws attention to how our position in relation to objects affects how we see them. Changing our position in relation to the models made on these two pages completely changes the picture we see.

Pages 94 Pop-up cards take children into paper engineering.

Pages 95 – 99 These shapes and picture patterns not only introduce children to the fitting of shapes together but are an early and very important introduction to the concept of area as amount of surface covered.

USING TOOLS SAFELY

A note to parents and teachers   *Tools make the work easier if you use the right tool for the right material. A parent or teacher should always supervise a child using a tool for the first time.*

Cardboard and paper   You will need several weights of paper and cardboard, from very thin paper for tracing to heavy cardboard for building sturdy things. To make the periscope, for example, you need cardboard the weight and strength of the back of a pad of paper. Many projects call for thinner cardboard, like an index card or a file folder, that will hold its shape but be flexible enough to bend into a circle.

Cutting cardboard and paper   A good pair of scissors will be enough for most of the projects in this book, but some really require using an *art knife* and a *metal* or *metal-edged ruler.*

An art knife is a pencil-sized blade holder that takes a single-edged sharp-pointed *No. 11 blade.* The blade must be very sharp, so handle it with care and replace it as soon as it starts to get dull.

Always use light pressure and several passes with the blade. Don't bear down and try to make the cut with one slice. Always work on a cutting surface large enough to hold the work completely. Remember that whatever is beneath your work will get cut too.

This kind of cutting is really very easy. Make sure that what you are going to cut is clearly marked. Tape it down to the cutting surface securely so that you don't have to worry about it slipping.

For very short cuts like those needed to make the slits for the Phenakistoscope or Zoetrope, you can hold the ruler by hand. For longer cuts clamp at least one end to the cutting surface.

Place the ruler on the line you want to cut. Hold the blade like a pencil against the edge of the ruler. Turn the blade edge very slightly toward the ruler. Pull the blade toward you the length of the cut several times until the cut is complete.

Always pull toward yourself. If you want to make a cut in another direction, turn the cardboard, not your wrist.

Scoring cardboard and paper   When paper or cardboard is too heavy for you to make a good, clean fold, then it needs to be scored. You can do this with a dull unpointed knife, like a butter knife, or a *stylus.*

You can make a stylus easily from a piece of dowel. Just sharpen it like a pencil and then cut or sand off the very sharp point so that it won't tear the paper you are scoring.

To score something, simply place your ruler against the line to be scored and drag the stylus point along the edge of the ruler. Use enough pressure to make a clearly visible mark, but not enough to tear.

If the stylus doesn't work then make a very light cut down the fold line with an art knife. Use very light

pressure and be sure not to cut all the way through the cardboard.

Once you've scored something, hold the ruler firmly on the fold line and fold up against it.

Making and using templates   A template is like a stencil that you create to draw the same thing over and over again. If you make it out of something heavy enough, you can even use it as a guide for scoring or cutting.

Working with balsa wood   Balsa is a very light soft wood that floats and is easy to work with. You can cut it like cardboard with an art knife, saw it with a small, fine-toothed saw, or whittle it. If you use an art knife, you will probably want to get one with a few assorted knife and saw blades and a blade clamp slightly larger than an art knife's. Get advice from a hobby shop on handles and blades.

Observe common-sense safety rules. Clamp your work down if you are cutting with a knife or a saw. Remember that the saw does its work as you push it away from you, but the knife cuts as you pull it.

When you whittle something, always hold the object above where you are working and whittle away from your hand and body.

Sawing wood, candles, and ballpoint pens   Working with a handsaw is very easy if you have the proper saw and if you use a vise or clamps to hold the object firm and steady.

For very soft or hard items a hacksaw with fine teeth is easiest to use and cleanest. Firmly secure the item with a vise or clamps and saw with even strokes putting pressure on the down stroke.

If you do not have a bench vise in your work area,

you can buy a portable one that clamps to any board or you can use C-clamps. Be sure that you do not work on a good table and that you protect the surface you are working on by putting scraps of wood or cardboard between the clamps and the table.

When using *clamps on a round object*, you will get a firmer grip if you clamp two identical items (dowels, candles, pens, etc.) at the same time. Put the two items down with several inches between them, lay a stiff block of wood across them, and then clamp the block down between the two items.

Before you saw a section off a disposable ballpoint, you need to remove the ink tube from the middle. Grab the metal tip of the pen with a pair of pliers and twist it back and forth until you can pull it out easily.

Cutting tin, plastic containers and tennis balls   You will need *tin snips* to cut up a tin can. It is easy to use them but be very careful because they are designed to cut heavy things and you do not want to nick your finger.

To cut a can, first remove the ends with a can opener and then cut down the can near the seam. Flatten the tin, turn it around and cut the seam off and throw it away. You now have a flat piece of tin to drill, cut, or shape as you wish.

Wear work gloves and be very careful of the sharp edges.

If you are cutting a plastic container, it is easier if you first remove the neck, which is usually heavier than the body of the container. Hold the body of the container braced between two blocks of wood that have been clamped to your work surface. Then use a hacksaw or other fine-toothed saw to do the job.

Once the neck is removed, you can cut the container easily with a pair of tin snips. If you are cutting a bottle down the center and the bottom is too heavy for the snips, cut up to the bottom and then bend it back and forth along the line you want to cut until the snips will do it easily.

To cut an old tennis ball in half use a very sharp knife with a short blade. Hold the ball firmly and cut down and away from your hand.

Using a power drill   Power drills are easy and safe to use if you follow a few simple precautions. Never use more than medium pressure with this tool. Let the drill do the work. Never use it around water or on anything wet.

Be sure that the item you are working on is secured so that it cannot slip. Place a piece of scrap wood behind it that you can drill into. Start your hole with a nail and run the drill slowly at first. Once you are sure the drill won't slip, increase the speed.

Never hold anything in your hand or rest it on your lap to drill it.

Never try to hold something secure with one hand while you drill with the other.

INDEX

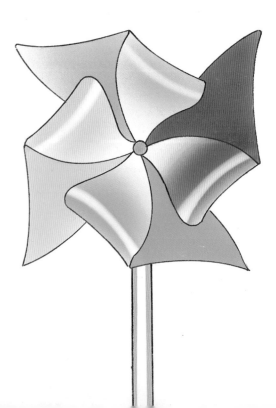